FUTURE
LIVES

BOOKS BY GLORIA CHADWICK

Discovering Your Past Lives

Spirituality and Self-Empowerment

Somewhere Over the Rainbow: A Soul's Journey Home

Reincarnation and Your Past-Life Memories

The Key to Self-Empowerment

Soul Shimmers: Awakening Your Spiritual Self

Happy Ways to Heal the Earth

Life Is Just a Dream

Psychic Senses: How to Develop Your Innate Powers

Inner Journeys: Meditations and Visualizations

How to Write Your Book and Get it Published the Write Way

The Path to Publishing Your Book

FUTURE
LIVES

Discovering and Understanding
Your Destiny

By Gloria Chadwick

STERLING

New York / London
www.sterlingpublishing.com

Revised portions of "The Game of Life" and "Tapestry of Life" from *Somewhere Over the Rainbow: A Soul's Journey Home* ©1992 by Gloria Chadwick are reprinted with permission from Mystical Mindscapes.

To learn more about the author, visit chadwickpages.com.

STERLING and the distinctive Sterling logo are registered trademarks of Sterling Publishing Co., Inc.

Library of Congress Cataloging-in-Publication Data

Chadwick, Gloria.
   Future lives : discovering & understanding your destiny / Gloria Chadwick.
      p. cm.
   Includes index.
   ISBN-13: 978-1-4027-4364-1
   ISBN-10: 1-4027-4364-5
   1. Future life. 2. Karma. 3. Reincarnation. 4. Precognition. I. Title.

BL535.C43 2008
202'.37--dc22

                              2007042276

10 9 8 7 6 5 4 3 2 1

Published by Sterling Publishing Co., Inc.
387 Park Avenue South, New York, NY 10016
© 2008 by Gloria Chadwick
Distributed in Canada by Sterling Publishing
C/o Canadian Manda Group, 165 Dufferin Street
Toronto, Ontario, Canada M6K 3H6
Distributed in the United Kingdom by GMC Distribution Services
Castle Place, 166 High Street, Lewes, East Sussex, England BN7 1XU
Distributed in Australia by Capricorn Link (Australia) Pty. Ltd.
P.O. Box 704, Windsor, NSW 2756, Australia

Book design and layout by Susan Fazekas

Manufactured in the United States of America
All rights reserved

Sterling ISBN-13: 978-1-4027-4364-1
            ISBN-10: 1-4027-4364-5

For information about custom editions, special sales, premium and corporate purchases, please contact Sterling Special Sales Department at 800-805-5489 or specialsales@sterlingpublishing.com.

This book is dedicated to my daughters Jennifer and Jaime, special souls that I've traveled with in many lifetimes.

Thanks to Stacy Prince, for suggesting the idea for this book.

Thanks to my agent, Linda Konner, for finding a home for this book.

Thanks to my editor, Jo Fagan, for your humor and help along the way.

Thanks to Cathlyn Matracia, for your insightful comments during the editing process.

Thanks to Cesar Cardenas, for talking me through fixing my computer when the normal template went corrupt and all my words were lost.

And mostly, thanks to all my wonderful students and clients who shared their experiences with me.

The time is now
and the
moment
is here.

Contents

All your lives are lived at the same time in various vibrations of energy. Shift your focus of awareness and frame of attention to meet yourself in past and future lifetimes, and to become aware of your probable selves. Interact with yourself in other lives to share knowledge and to become aware of events and experiences that influence your present reality in unseen and unexpected ways. Balancing karma. See how you change and create the past and the future in the present. See how the souls you're connected with now appear as past and future people. Interactive Exercises: Meeting Yourself. Soul-Expanding Meditations: Rainbow Energies. Significant Past-Future Souls.

If you could pull the future into the present, what would you do with what you learned and how would it affect you? What would you bring back from the future as a gift to yourself in the present? What corresponding changes would ripple through the past, present, and future? See how your present experiences, and your past ones, would change to support and frame your future experiences. Dream-weaving. Mind-Opening Meditation: Multicolored Pictures and Patterns. Look into future lives to observe your soul patterns and to see the talents and abilities you have, then weave them into both the present and the past.

You already know how to see your future. Images of the future often show themselves in dreams, intuition, and precognition. Does the future exist within the present? Empty Energy. Explains why the future appears to be vague and misty. Putting energy into motion by putting your feelings into the future. Interactive Experience: Following Your Future.

We're all travelers through time, journeying through our many multidimensional experiences. Somewhere-Nowhere.You didn't just appear out of nowhere, did you? Neither did your experiences. Their origins were created somewhere before, at some other place in time. The true meaning of nowhere. Eternity stretches far beyond what the mind can reach. Some common fears about facing the future. Traps and trip-ups to be aware of. Entering the void of time. Interactive Experience: Being Here, There, Everywhere, and Nowhere. The ever-present here and now. Cycles and connections. Rhythm of Reincarnation. The beginning and the end. Interactive Experience: Alpha/Omega. Your very own time-travel machine.

Introduction

Ever since time began—whenever that was, it was such a long time ago that I can't really remember it—people have been pondering the mysteries of time. From time to time, we've all thought about how time really works. Perhaps at one time or another, you've experienced time in a structure different than past, present, and future—yesterday was, today is, and tomorrow will be. At times, maybe all the vibrations of past, present, and future blended together.

Maybe because of the experiences in your life when time refused to fit into a nice, neat, logical explanation, you began to wonder about time, and maybe you decided to look into it more thoroughly. In doing so, maybe you began to change your focus of awareness to fit your experiences; and you found that time didn't hold true to linear, limited vibrations of past, present, and future.

Being curious about time myself, since I've purposely placed myself into many of my past lives and inadvertently tripped into a few of my future lives, I thought it would be interesting to deeply explore the energy expressions of time as they relate to the vibrations of our experiences in all of our past, present, and future lives.

Many of my past-life regression clients have looked into their future lives while they were exploring issues in a past life that affected their present life. They found that their future lives had just as much, if not more, influence on their present life—showing them that the future creates the past and the present just as much as the past creates the present and the future.

Simultaneously looking into and living in all of your past, present, and future lives, can be illuminating and enlightening; it offers us the opportunity to stretch our awareness and expand our horizons. It enables us to see more of ourselves and to get a clearer, more complete picture of our experiences—to see how they happen, to understand why they happen, and to become aware of what we can do about them now—how we can influence and change aspects of them in the past, the present, and the future, if we choose.

As I begin this book—right here, right now, in the present—I have a feeling that the words have already been written, and I'm reading them from a future script in my mind, seeing the words that I've written at some other point and place in time, and putting them on paper so you can read them, too. I wonder where this book will take me and what it will show me. I wonder what the words will really say, and, at the same time, part of me already knows because I've been there before, even though I haven't yet arrived.

By now you may be thinking, Wait a minute. Let me read that last paragraph again, perhaps because it didn't make any sense or maybe because it makes *perfect* sense. By the time you read it again, you've experienced the past, the present, and the future, all right here, right now, captured in one small paragraph. If you can relate that concept of time to all your experiences, you'll see that at every moment in your life, you're always in the present, even when it appears that you were remembering the past or looking into the future.

This book is based on thirty-five years of personal experience and on the experiences of my students and hypnosis clients. It does not reflect a scientific study of time, nor is it intended to be a comprehensive coverage of the many theories of time. It merely relates what I've discovered about how time works in relationship to past, present, and future lives, and the conclusions I've drawn. Better minds than mine have looked into the nature of time and been baffled by the subtle quirks and mysterious expressions of it. Even Einstein had difficulty with it. I'm no expert, just a soul journeying through my Earth experiences in physical form trying to see how time really works by understanding how it relates to the experiences in my life.

This book offers a redefinition of a past-life point of view about reincarnation; it's centered in the present and woven into all the interrelated aspects of past and future events that your soul is in the process of experiencing. It offers you ways to explore various vibrations of time—to look into your past, present, and future lives—and to draw your own conclusions based on what you experience in different dimensions of time.

The way you view and experience time will be influenced to a certain extent by your thoughts and beliefs and what you've previously read or heard about. As you read this book and explore the ideas and concepts it contains, keep an open mind; listen to your thoughts and feelings, and follow your interpretations.

Try not to separate your thoughts into past, present, and future vibrations of time; keep your thoughts synchronized with the experiences in your present life to see for yourself how time operates. Simultaneous time can be a bit abstract; there's nothing concrete about it. Logic doesn't mix well with abstraction. If you try to view time logically in order to fit it into a concrete frame of reality, you'll end up with a huge headache, because time isn't logical. Keep in mind that everything is relative and can be easily understood by applying it to what you experience in your explorations of time.

If you get a little lost or confused as you thread your way through the mysteries of time and space, simply change your focus of awareness and frame of mind—your perspectives and perceptions—to fit what you are experiencing with time. You'll find that doing so will show you the truth about time. Look at your past and future lives in relation to your present life to ground yourself in the present and give you a firm foothold into both the past and the future.

The key to unlocking the mysteries of simultaneous, synchronous time is to be centered in the present, in the eternal NOW. Watch how time vibrates in the present as it flows in, around, and through your experiences—to see how it affects your present life and influences your past and future lives. I'd like to offer you a wonderful adventure. Turn the page and travel through time. Expand your outlook and open your insights. Journey to higher horizons and visit new vistas. Explore all the vibrations of your experiences—right here, right now. I invite you to see through the present to look into the time-spaces of *all* your lives—past, present, and future.

°
ˈ

ONE

Reviewing Reincarnation

D o you ever wonder what your future lives hold for you? Are you just a little curious about what's going to happen in both the future in this life and your future lives because of what you do in this life and what you've done in past lives? Do you wish there were a way you could somehow zip through the vibrations of time and space to get a preview of what's going to occur?

While you can catch glimpses of the future through dreams, intuition, and precognition—these are viable avenues that we'll explore later in this book—there is another way. You can look into the events in your future lives—here and now—by going with the flow of time and by redefining reincarnation and looking at karma and past lives in a new light.

How do time and reincarnation operate in your reality? The most commonly accepted definition of reincarnation is that over eons, a soul repeatedly incarnates into different physical bodies in consecutive lifetimes for the purposes of acquiring knowledge and balancing karma, with the goals of attaining enlightenment and perfecting one's soul. Your past actions (karma) cause and create the present events and emotions in your life. While this interpretation of reincarnation offers you the opportunity to balance your karma and grow your soul, the basic definition says that you live one life at a time and that each life is experienced in a linear timeframe of past, present, and future.

This definition doesn't sound complete; it sounds as if you're stuck somewhere in the present, tossed about by the winds of fate, at the mercy of whatever your karma is. If you stretch your memory, you can look into the past, but this limiting definition doesn't give you a way to see into the future, because the future hasn't happened yet. It says that the past is past; it's over and done with; all you have now is the present and a vague future that looms somewhere in the misty beyond. This gives you power in the present, in the form of your free will, to make choices about how you want to work with and balance your karma, and how it may play out in the future, both in this lifetime and in a future life.

Once you've either corrected or changed your karma, the definition then turns around to limit your power because it doesn't let you do anything with a future lifetime, except to wonder what's going to happen to you because of your actions in this lifetime and what you may carry over from a past life. There are events and emotions in your past lives that don't affect you now because the circumstances aren't right, but they will affect you in a future life when the opportunity arises.

However, inherent in the definition of reincarnation is that you can remember your past-life experiences in your present life and use the knowledge and understanding you gain from looking within your past-life memories to help you balance your karma in the present in a positive manner. Remembering events in your past lives also provides you with answers to the questions of what you did in past lives and why you're involved in whatever it is that you're experiencing now.

Even if you can't remember any events in your past lives, you don't need to know what your karma is to balance it. Just take a good look at what your life is showing you, and you'll see the energies of past events that you've experienced as they repeat themselves in the present. By balancing present events, you simultaneously balance the energies of events in your past lives, clearing up the karma.

Karma is energy in motion. It's the replaying of events and emotions from your past lives in the present. When the right circumstances merge, the energy vibrations of your karma, which is created by your actions from the past, shows itself in a similar experience in the present. This is because the past and present energies are synchronized into what you're experiencing now. But that's only the half of it. Because your past and present experiences are composed of energy vibrations, as you change the energy of your past experiences—your karma—in the present, you simultaneously change and create the energies of your present and future experiences.

Any thought, feeling, or experience you change in your life now will interact with and correspondingly change all the interrelated thoughts, feelings, and experiences in every lifetime—past, present, and future—because the energies are all intertwined. Reincarnation, viewed from this perspective, shows you that you have the power to create and change anything you want in any of your past, present, and future lives.

Open up the concept of reincarnation a bit more and take a deeper look inside. Review reincarnation in a clearer, more complete manner. The word *review* means literally "to re-see." Look into and explore the idea that experiences in your past lives are more than a memory. What if they're events and situations in your present life that are experienced in a different vibration of energy and awareness, and you perceive them playing out in the form of a memory?

And what about the future? Maybe your past, present, and future lives aren't lived in linear, isolated frames of time. Maybe they're all vibrating together, in perfect harmony and synchronicity with one another. Maybe your future lives exist now, side by side, paralleling your past lives and present life in similar vibrations of energy that are only a thought away from your awareness and recognition.

Take this one step further. Look at reincarnation in reverse. What if time runs backward? What if your future lives happen first? What if events in your past lives are reflections of events in your future lives and are also caused and created by events in your present life? If events in your future lives happen first, then they cause and create the events in your past and present lives in the same way that you had previously thought of reincarnation as your past lives affecting your present life; your future lives weren't even in the picture. This flips the whole concept around of how we view reincarnation from a past-life point of view. It's very mind stretching, as well as freeing and empowering.

If you look at your past lives from an open, free-flowing frame of time, viewing reincarnation as the future happening first, it opens up a wide range of choices and possibilities, because it gives you the opportunity to do more than just balance your karma by changing the present energy vibrations of past experiences. It gives you the power to change the energies of events in your past lives before they happen, because their beginnings were created in the future instead of in the past.

You can go yet further by expanding your outlook and opening up your insights to see a more complete view. Instead of the future creating your present and your past, consider the idea that your past lives and present life, instead of creating your future lives, are actually part of your future lives. You could then change the energies of the future, too, in your present life. This gives you another realm to explore, but you can go even one step further.

What if you live in your past, present, and future lives at the same time in different spaces and vibrations of energy? What if your past, present, and future lives are all happening simultaneously? Take a moment or two to wrap your mind around that concept. This way of looking at reincarnation is what this book is based on; it's where we go from here as we take a trip through time.

The simultaneous time-space concept opens up a whole new world and shows you a complete picture that provides you with a way of seeing how your past karma, and the way you balance it in the present to change the energies of your past experiences, plays out in the future. At the same time you're seeing that, you're looking into your future lives to see both the effect that the changed experiences have on your past and present lives, and how the future karma you've incurred also plays out in the present and the past. You see how and why your past and future karma is showing itself now by looking through the reflections of experiences in your present life.

This view offers an all-encompassing, comprehensive way to see inside reincarnation because it shows you that incorporated within your present life are all the experiences and emotions in what appear to be your past and future lives. This fits in perfectly with the original definition of reincarnation, which says that the present is all there is, because the past and the future are really part of the present. This sounds like a much more complete definition of reincarnation.

This way of looking at reincarnation isn't new. In fact, it's probably as old as time itself. Broaden your horizons a bit more and focus your awareness into a larger picture. If you live in your past, present, and future lives simultaneously, then you're living more than one life at the same time somewhere else in other spaces and vibrations of time. Maybe you haven't been looking at the whole picture.

Reincarnation doesn't paint a stagnant, still-life picture. It's a constantly moving, vibrant, ever-changing experience. Reincarnation is life in motion, and time moves within and through and around the energy vibrations of all your past-present-future experiences. To draw an analogy, look at life as an ocean with waves of time that wash up on the shore and return to the ocean. The waves of time ebb and flow in a rhythmic pattern that repeats itself over and over; it's the same with your experiences.

If you look at life only in the present, you're standing on the shore watching the waves. As you balance your karma from the past, you begin to wade and splash through the waves, getting your feet wet. But life has a way of showing you things you need to see and sometimes those waves wash up on shore with tides and undercurrents that pull you out to sea when the energies of karma flow into your life. As the waves flow to the rhythm of the ocean—as your experiences flow to the rhythm of your life—they go into the past, the present, and the future.

Any movement on your part—a change of thought or feeling or experience in your life—will change the motion of the waves and the direction of your experiences into another vibration. By shifting your focus of attention—your perceptions and perspectives—or changing your experiences, you shift the motion and direction of your life.

As you take another look into the complete concept of reincarnation, and you see what your life shows you, you'll see that you have all the power in the world and the universe to create and change anything in the way that you want to in all of your past, present, and future lives. Jump in; the water's fine. Reexperience reincarnation in a new way that's meaningful to you by redefining it. Rewrite the scenes and scenarios in all your past, present, and future lives, either singly or simultaneously. The truth inside the definition of reincarnation will remain the same, no matter which way you look at it.

TWO

Past, Present, and Future

Time is an elusive concept that slips and slides through explanations, defying labels that limit its true essence and expression. Time, if singled out and studied logically in a linear format, loses all the characteristics and qualities that make it uniquely what it is—time. To understand time as it really is, look at it in its natural form.

Time is a fluid vibration of energy that moves in all directions at once as it flows into every aspect of your experiences—as the energy of time flows through space and affects the motions of matter. Time isn't locked into a framework of clocks and calendars, schedules and appointments. Time is open and free; it's mysterious and magical. Yet time will show you what it's all about if you just see it for itself.

Time can be viewed from many perspectives and perceptions. The past, present, and future exist in different frameworks of awareness. We most often think of time in terms of past, present, and future—the past has already happened, the present is happening now, and the future has yet to happen. But, we've all had experiences that defy this traditional definition of time.

For example, we've all experienced events in our lives in which time didn't seem to exist or became distorted when we were totally involved in doing something we enjoy, such as reading a great book, watching a good movie, or being intensely involved in another activity. It seems that time just flew by and we lost all track of time and physical reality because we became so involved in and totally focused on what we were doing and experiencing that nothing else existed at the time, at least not in our perception. Hours may have passed, and we thought only a few minutes went by. In other situations, a minute can seem like hours. We've all had days in which time dragged on endlessly, such as when we're at work and watching the clock, just praying for 5:00. The same amount of time passed in both situations, but it seemed longer or shorter depending on our perception of it and our involvement with it.

When you dream, you are unaware of time, though time passes. In your dreams, time doesn't exist in a linear framework. Time is experienced out of its physical perspective. When you dream, you dream about the past, the present, and the future—all at the same time. They interweave and are happening as you experience them in your dream. Perhaps you've had a precognitive dream about something that was going to occur in the future. If the future hasn't happened yet, how do you know what's going to occur unless it is already in the process of occurring?

The same is true when you look into past-life memories. When you remember and reexperience a past-life memory, you blend the energies of the past and the present together into a current framework of time. The energies of time are interconnected between the past and the present, synchronized with the energies of that past-present experience. By the way, what holds true for delving into past lives is also true for looking into future lives.

The simultaneous time-space concept states that everything is occurring now—that the past, present, and future are happening simultaneously but in different vibrations of energy and different spaces of matter. Time is not perceived in linear blocks; time is a fluid movement of the present now.

Within the fluid energies of time, you can influence what you did in the past by changing your actions in the present, which will then alter the energies of what occurred in the past and modify what you experience in both the new, changed present and the future. It also changes what you have already experienced in the future because the future shapes and scripts the present as much as the past does. You can change your future after it has already happened and before it occurs. Ditto for the past.

If you accept this theory as true, or even as an interesting possibility, it gives you many choices and a tremendous amount of power in how you want to shape the energies of your past, present, and future experiences. For example, you can change the energies of what you did in a past life, thereby changing or altering what you will experience in the present because of the changed past, which will also influence, affect, and alter your future experiences. Nothing is written in stone; the energies of your thoughts, feelings, and actions influence and change all your interrelated experiences in the past, present, and future simultaneously.

If you've recalled any of your past lives, you've noticed that your past experiences don't sit still and stay in the past. As soon as you change your thoughts and feelings about the events in your past lives, and especially if you make changes through your actions in the present to balance your karma, you've seen how the vibrations of your past and present experiences began to affect the future in this life while simultaneously altering the energies and emotions of the past in the present.

Thoughts, feelings, and actions are composed of energy. Everything we think, feel, and do in the present has repercussions and reactions in the past and the future. As we think, feel, and act in the present, we influence all the interrelated vibrations of time. Whatever we change will correspondingly change all the events connected with that experience in the past, the present, and the future simultaneously. Everything is connected—the past, present, and future aren't separate; they're all part of the same vibration. They're woven together in and through the fabric of our life.

The present now incorporates the past, the present, and the future within itself.

The words *past, present,* and *future* are labels we attach to vibrations of energy and spaces of matter to help us differentiate and understand our experiences. This limits the expressions of what they really are. To show you how this works, look at your experiences as being intertwined on a flexible string, like the string on a harp. The bottom of the string represents the past, the middle represents the present, and the top represents the future. If you pluck the string at the bottom (past), it will cause the string to vibrate in the middle (present) and reverberate at the top (future), and vice versa. If you pluck the string in the center (present), it will simultaneously cause the top (future) and the bottom (past) to move in a corresponding vibratory motion. The vibrations are all tuned together and synchronized; they influence one another. All your experiences, your thoughts, and your feelings, every event and circumstance, are connected through the vibrations of energy that reach everywhere at once.

Look at time in a spiritual framework. Time is a vibration of energy, a dimension of space. On a nonphysical, spiritual level, time doesn't exist—because it's not needed to measure something that isn't of a physical nature. From this viewpoint, time serves as a convenience for those who reincarnate on the physical, three-dimensional Earth plane.

In the realm of spiritual reality, time is measured as a flowing movement with the synchronous past, present, and future all occupying motions of space simultaneously, but in a different dimension or vibration of energy. This resonance is similar to the different sounds you achieve when you pluck the string on the harp in different places. The vibrations of time interact with and influence all the energies, dimensions, and aspects of your experiences, because you're a physical and spiritual being at the same time.

Let's come back down to Earth for a moment. Let's be logical and look at time from a linear viewpoint. If I expect you to be open to the possibility that all your past, present, and future lives are happening simultaneously, in synchronicity with one another, and some are even happening in other dimensions and realities, the least I can do is go along with a more familiar perception and explore the idea that your past, present, and future lives are all happening separately in a linear framework of time.

With this in mind, let's suppose the past has already happened. Everything you thought, did, experienced, and felt before now is permanently etched somewhere, at some place and point in time, and can't be changed. All you can do is become aware of it and understand it to see how it relates to your present life, then use this understanding to help you in a positive way in the present.

The future, supposedly, hasn't happened yet. There seems to be nothing but potential energy swirling around in empty spaces. If we're curious about the future, we might try to take a peek to see what's there instead of just wondering what the future holds. We'll look deeply into the future later in this book. For now, let's focus on the present to see what it's all about.

For the sake of clarity (and for this chapter), let's suppose that the present is everything you're experiencing in your life at this very moment, right now in this place and at this time. A lot of people think that the present covers today, this week, this month, this year, or even this entire lifetime. To be really logical, the present hardly exists; it's barely here at all. It's just a teeny, tiny point in time, a little blip of eternity, barely a second. Blink your eyes and it's gone forever, faded into the past as it flows into the future.

Let's say that the present covers more than one second because our thoughts are continuously in the past or the future, in a memory, or in plans for something we'd like to do or something that's happening now that we'd like to change or bring about in the future. We seem to place the present somewhere else all the time. Some of us tend to live in the past, reminiscing about the good old days, or looking through our memories, searching to find a reason for something that's occurring now or to uncover a clue that will help us understand a current problem.

Just as many of us seem to be drawn to the future. We talk a lot about our goals and the things we'd like to do, such as, "When I get my raise or a promotion, I'll do this or that," or, "Two months from now, I'll be in Hawaii enjoying my vacation." It appears that we're never here now in the present; we always seem to be somewhere else in our past or our future.

The past and the future are so much a part of the present that it's difficult to keep them separate. Centering your attention and focusing your awareness into this one particular second or into one particular experience appears to be next to impossible. Your mind wanders off in all directions at once, going into related thoughts and changing the subject all the time, similar to how the vibrations of the past, present, and future intertwine in our experiences.

That reminds me of something one of my teachers asked me to do to show me how hard it is to think of only one thing at a time. She asked me to think of a rose—just a rose and nothing else, for one minute. I thought of a rose for one minute. During that minute, I also thought about the fragrance of a rose. I thought about the color. I remembered how velvety and smooth the petals felt. I thought about the rose bushes in my garden and wondered when the buds were going to bloom. I thought of how pretty they'd look. I recalled the first time someone sent me roses. I see what my teacher meant. In that one minute, my thoughts, while related to a rose, were all over the place. They were in the past, the present, and the future simultaneously.

Try this for yourself. Think of a rose and nothing else. Notice how many interrelated thoughts, images, and feelings come into your mind. It's the same way with the vibrations of your experiences in your past, present, and future lives.

We got sidetracked. Let's get back to the present. This is, supposedly, where we really live; and seeing things as they are, or as they seem to be, we see that the past *was*, the present *is*, and the future *will be*. This is what we base our real-life reality on. With those linear and limiting definitions, we have a huge past, a very small but powerful present, and an empty future that waits for us somewhere in the vague beyond. Are we seeing all there is to see, or are we looking at only a small part of a much larger picture? Maybe all those interrelated images and thoughts from the past and the future are trying to tell us something.

INTERACTIVE EXERCISE: BACK TO THE FUTURE

Let's suppose the future is in front of you and the past is behind you; let's pretend your past lives have already happened. What would you do if you could create a new real-life reality by changing and rearranging the energies of events and emotions in your past lives while simultaneously influencing your experiences and feelings in the present and the future?

We'll explore this deeply in Chapter Five and look at it in reverse from the future in Chapter Nine. For now let's stay in the present to show you how this works by focusing on a past event in your present life that played out in the future. You'll be going into the past, present, and future in this lifetime to see how the energies of time vibrate and ripple through interconnected experiences. You can change and rearrange the energy of a past event to shape and support what you'd like to experience now in your present and future real-life realities. You might even see how the future creates your past and your present.

How many times have you said to yourself, "If I knew then what I know now"? Here's your chance to find out. Think of a present-day experience that you'd like to change because you don't like the way it played out, or a choice or decision you made that you wish would have turned out differently.

In your thoughts, go into the past, back to the beginning where it started in this life. Bring the memory of it into your mind. Really put your feelings into it. Become emotionally involved all over again. Re-create and reexperience it in your mind, with all the feelings and thoughts that were originally there. See how it played out all the way through from beginning to end, from the past, through the present, into the future, which is now. Be in touch with all your past, present, and future feelings. Watch how everything that happened in the past, and your emotions about it, influences and interacts with what occurred in the present and the future.

From this future viewpoint (where you are now and knowing all the various elements of what you experienced), see how your situation moves backward from the future (the outcome) through the present, into the past (to the point of origin), and how it re-created your future (which you're experiencing now). Notice all the interactions between your past, present, and future thoughts, feelings, and actions.

Look at how your future (the outcome) created your past so you could experience your present, so you could then reexperience your future (which is happening now). Notice how your past thoughts and actions created your present. Look into your past feelings that created the future outcome of what you're experiencing now, and you'll see that the future of this situation—the, outcome—is what actually caused the situation to occur in the past because of your future feelings which put your past thoughts into action.

Now, change your thoughts and feelings about the present situation (the outcome) in any way you choose, to see how this situation would have played out in the past, and how it would be in the present, if you'd had the future awareness then that you have now. Change, rearrange, create, re-create, or un-create the scenes in your mind. Watch how all your choices play out in the present and see how things are different. Just use your imagination and a bit of logic. Stay closely connected to the situation, or you might tend to go off in too many different directions at once. (We'll do that later in the book; but for now, do one thing at a time. It's easier and less brain-boggling!)

You might be surprised to find that your feelings have changed about the original event, along with the scenes of the situation you changed in your mind. This exercise shows you how you can rearrange the energy of the past from the future to shape and support what you'd like to experience now, and to also change and re-vibrate the energies of what you've already experienced and will experience in the future.

You may be even more surprised when you see the effects of what you've done reflected in the future. At the same time that you changed the energy vibrations of your past experience, through your thoughts and feelings about it, you created and changed events—in direct proportion to the now-changed situation—in both the present and the future as it relates to this one particular experience.

Maybe you're not convinced that the past, the present, and the future are all vibrating in the same interconnected wave of energy or that you've changed the past and rearranged the future in the present. Nothing is really different, except for your feelings. It was just a mental maneuver, a game, a way to play with your imagination. But what if it's more than that? What if it's real? Only time will tell. Even though it may not seem real at this point in time, continue to watch this now-changed situation as it plays out in the present and see what unfolds in the future (from the present now). When the future catches up to the present, you may discover that it's more real than it appears to be right now.

All your experiences are limited only by your thoughts, feelings, and beliefs, by where you focus your attention and center your awareness. Think about it. You can experience, change, rearrange, create, re-create, and un-create the events and emotions in your past, present, and future lives—right here, right now—in the timeless energy of your mind.

While you're waiting for the future to happen, here's something else for you to think about. What you did in the above exercise is similar to what you do between physical lives when you're creating the situations and circumstances you want to experience in your next incarnation. You're working with the awareness that you wish you'd had then, now. (We're still supposing that the past, present, and future, as well as the interim between lives, occur in a linear format.)

When you reincarnate, you put this spiritual awareness and inner knowing into your subconscious mind. When the time and place are right, a particular situation that you've created and/or chosen to experience occurs. When this situation shows itself in your present life, you have the opportunity to change and rearrange the energy of the past, just as you did in the interactive exercise. All you need to do is open up your inner knowing—your spiritual awareness—to see things as they really are.

THREE

Karma and
Creating Your Own Reality

K arma is the replaying of events and emotions from past lives that you're now experiencing in the present. Creating your own reality is the concept that you create everything you experience through your words, thoughts, feelings, beliefs, ideas, imagination, actions, and reactions. Both karma and creating your own reality operate under the universal Law of Balance, which is more commonly referred to as cause and effect. Applied to the philosophy of reincarnation, balance strives to make wrong things right, to even them out and bring them into harmony. It's self-correcting and cyclical; it returns to itself over and over, in a rhythmic pattern that repeats itself in similar experiences to achieve balance. Karma and creating your own reality work together to bring the energies of your experiences into balance.

However, there's more going on than first meets the eye. While it appears that karma was originally created (cause) in a past life that is now showing itself (effect) in your present life, it also appears that as you create your reality (cause) in the present, you're creating the karma (effect) that you'll experience either later in this life or in a future life. It looks as if karma and creating your own reality are basically the same thing; the only difference is the labels of *past* and *present* that are attached to them. Look at karma and creating your own reality from different perspectives and time frames. A shift of focus or a change of perception in your thoughts can reveal aspects of karma and creating your own reality that perhaps you weren't aware of before.

Consider a few fundamentals of karma and creating your own reality. Both originate in your thoughts and feelings, and both show the results of how you respond and react to the situations you encounter and the actions you put into motion. Your current experiences show the energy vibrations of your previous thoughts, feelings, actions, and reactions in motion. Your thoughts and feelings change your life and create the rhythm of your reality.

Both karma and creating your own reality stress responsibility for your actions and the importance of accepting the consequences for everything you've created. This empowers and enables you to make choices and changes. Because your experiences are created in your mind and in your emotions before they appear in your life, you can change the direction and expression of your experiences simply by changing your thoughts and feelings. Your experiences will then reflect those changes.

Karmic situations appear in your life when the time is right for balancing, when something similar in your present life sets the energies of a past-life event into motion. In the framework of creating your own reality in this life, look into your current experiences, and you'll see how they reflect your previous actions and your earlier thoughts and feelings. It's the same with karma, except that karma was created in a past lifetime, not the present one.

Karma shows the earlier energies of your experiences that are now in motion. When you look at your experiences from a linear time frame of past, present, and future, you see that your present karma reflects your past actions. From this perspective, it *seems* that the only thing you can do with your karma now is to just let it play out and experience it, while doing your best to balance it in the process. This gives you the opportunity to understand your karma—and why it is happening—and to change your thoughts and feelings, thereby changing your present experiences. This is where creating your own reality comes into the picture.

Creating your own reality puts your free will into motion. You have free will to make choices—choices about how you want to change your present experiences through your current thoughts, feelings, and actions. Your choices create your current and future circumstances, just as your past choices have created your past experiences and present karma. It *seems* that creating your own reality only gives you control over your present thoughts and feelings. The thoughts, feelings, and actions that created your karma can't be changed, just understood and balanced. Your past feelings *appear* to be untouchable and your future feelings *appear* to be unreachable.

Notice the words *seems* and *appear* in the previous paragraphs. If you let go of linear time limits and look at karma and creating your own reality in the framework of simultaneous time and synchronicity, you'll see that your free will to make choices that will change the experiences in your life—whether it is your past, present, or future life—is not limited in any way. Only your physical body is limited to the present space and time.

This is a good thing, because where in the world would you be without your body? You'd probably be floating off somewhere in space traveling through the energy vibrations of time—maybe in the middle of what appears to be a dreamlike excursion into a future life or a different life in another dimension, exploring the past and the future simultaneously, and discovering lots of very interesting and intriguing things about your soul and your experiences.

Time doesn't matter in the energy of your mind; the energies of your thoughts, feelings, and experiences transcend time because your awareness exists in the framework of spiritual energy even when you're in physical form. Both karma and creating your own reality are based on choices. You have the power within you now to change previous choices and to create present and future choices on a more aware, enlightened level of mind simply by shifting the focus of your attention and opening up your spiritual awareness to clearly see the whole picture. You can create and change the past and the future in the present because the past and the future are happening simultaneously right now.

The key is to place the focus of your awareness into the timeless energy of your mind—into your thoughts and feelings—and to change your experiences based on the complete picture by putting yourself inside your experiences and really feeling their interconnected, simultaneous vibrations. The following interactive exercise shows how this works. (A detailed explanation and exploration of getting into the vibe of simultaneous time and synchronizing your awareness with it is covered in Chapter Six.)

INTERACTIVE EXERCISE:
CREATING KARMA

Before you engage in the interactive exercise, here are a few more things to consider: Creating your own reality and balancing your karma in the present will shape and form your future experiences as it simultaneously reshapes and reforms the vibrations of your experiences in the past, and vice versa. That's not all it does. This exercise can help you understand how the energies of past, present, and future experiences vibrate together and are interwoven into every aspect of your life. You may even see how the future creates and shapes the past through karma.

The past is an integral part of the present because the energy of past experiences intertwines with the energy of present experiences. The energy surrounding previous events remains even after the event is over. You can influence the energies of events that have occurred, which will also affect and influence all interrelated energies within those events, even as the vibrations simultaneously affect and alter the present and the future. As you change things in the past, those changed energies will ripple through your present, changing your present experiences while also affecting, changing, creating, and un-creating the energies of your future experiences.

Past: *Think about a situation you were involved in yesterday and what you did or didn't do in the situation. Choose a situation that you feel emotionally connected to. It can be either a positive or a negative experience. Notice your thoughts and feelings about it. See how the situation originated, what you did to cause it to occur or the part you played in bringing it into your life. Label this* Karma.

Present: *Look at how yesterday's experience is affecting you today in your thoughts and feelings, and as it shows itself in your current situation, look at what you're doing about it now in your thoughts, feelings, actions, reactions, and responses. Label this* Creating Your Own Reality.

Near Future: *Tomorrow, notice how both your karma and creating your own reality are currently affecting you and what is happening in this past-present-future situation. Look back over the last three days to see how you've experienced the past in the present to create your future, all in the time frame of just a few days.*

Karma/Creating Your Own Reality: *Get adventurous with karma. Choose a situation in your present life that indicates karma is in motion. Give it some careful thought to see what you've done in the past that caused your karma to show itself in the present. If you're not aware of what created your karma, just imagine a hypothetical happening in what could be a past life* based on your present situation. Look for similarities to your present situation. These are the interweaving threads of energy that pull the past and present together.

In your mind—your inner knowing—carry this karmic situation over the span of several weeks (or lifetimes), looking at your actions and reactions, noting your thoughts and feelings, in each individual experience relating to this situation to see how karma replays itself and how it actually becomes creating your own reality. Pay special attention to how both the past and the present affect your future.

You might notice how continuous and circular time is, and how situations tend to repeat themselves until they're either corrected or changed by you creating another expression for the energy of the situation to show itself in. This helps you understand how the Law of Balance operates in your experiences and how it applies to everything in your life, whether it began as karma or creating your own reality.

This exercise also explains the whole philosophy of reincarnation and why reincarnation occurs. There's more that this exercise can show you. If you look deeply into what you experienced by watching your situation unfold and express itself, you'll see how and why chances and coincidences happen, and you'll get a glimpse of how simultaneous time and synchronicity operate. You'll see how you synchronize all your experiences into the rhythm of your reality through the waves of time.

Far Future: To see how the future flows into and through the vibrations of time, work with the outcome of the karmic situation or imagine a hypothetical happening in the future based on your present situation. From this viewpoint, see how the future situation moves backward into the present and the past.

If you look closely, you might see that your future created and shaped your past so you could experience your present, so you could then reexperience your future, which has already happened.

How do you want to label the future? Karma? Or Creating Your Own Reality? *Or perhaps you see that by creating your present-past from the future, you're working with the awareness that you wish you'd had then, now. (Refer to the interactive exercise in Chapter Two.) All your feelings and experiences are limited only by your thoughts and beliefs. Think about it. You're creating your past-present-future reality, and your corresponding karma—right here, right now—in the timeless energy of your mind.*

THE GAME OF LIFE

Stretch your awareness and look into all the multidimensional aspects of karma and creating your own reality. Creating your reality through your thoughts, feelings, actions, reactions, and beliefs creates the karmic experiences you have in your past, present, and future lives. Your experiences can go every which way, depending on your thoughts, feelings, actions, and reactions, and by what your soul creates for you to experience—what you created for yourself in a higher vibration of awareness and knowing.

A few of the reasons we reincarnate, aside from balancing the karma we've set into motion, is because our souls desire the adventure of an Earth experience, a change of environment. We like being in physical form in the manifest world of energy. We like to play with physical energy and practice the art of creation while we advance our awareness into ever-higher levels of knowledge and enlightenment through earthly experiences.

What if reincarnation is really a game we play to ultimately discover the true nature of energy and the reality of our soul? How would the game play out? Here's what I think: The thoughts, feelings, and actions that created your experiences would drift through time and space and appear in your life when your vibrations were most in tune with them and say, "Surprise; you created me and now here I am."

It would be like playing a game called This is Your Life: Understanding the Illusions of Your Reality. There are lots of twists and turns in the form of fate and different paths to follow, but the purpose of the game is to completely understand all your experiences on every level of energy and awareness and to evolve your soul. In the course of the game, you have to gather all the energy expressions of your karma by picking up the pieces of your experiences and balancing them by putting them into their proper places and perspectives.

There are different levels of skill and lots of choices. You earn credits or debits, depending on how you play the game. To move forward, you have to completely immerse yourself in your feelings and learn from all your experiences. You're not supposed to cheat, but you can if you want to. If you cheat, or if you refuse to learn, you have to go back and do those experiences all over again.

You're allowed to use hindsight, insight, and foresight to help you only if you believe what you see in those images. You choose how to play the game by creating any reality you want, but you do have to follow a few rules. First, you create and choose all your experiences and your responses to them. There are no accidents. You do everything on purpose.

Second, all your thoughts and feelings, actions and reactions, manifest into karmic expressions of energy in one reality or another, whether you're aware of them or not.

Third, time doesn't exist in linear spaces of past, present, and future. Everything occurs simultaneously in perfect synchronicity.

Fourth, all your experiences are connected through vibrations of energy. Each and every one of your experiences influences all your other interrelated experiences, either directly or indirectly. If you change anything in your life, then everything even remotely related to or associated with that particular thing changes proportionately—even things that have already happened.

Seeing the illusions of your reality is one thing; watching the energy of your thoughts, feelings, and actions appear in your life is something else. It's a matter of seeing how time vibrates and how energy really works as it manifests into your experiences. That's what makes the game fun and interesting. To win the game and put all the pieces together, you have to completely understand all your experiences in every vibration of energy on every level of reality, both seen and unseen, by synchronizing their energy expressions with your spiritual awareness.

After you've balanced and put all the energy expressions of your thoughts, feelings, and experiences into their proper places and perspectives of time, space, matter, and motion, you know everything there is to know about your soul and what life is really all about. You have a complete picture of your soul.

Is the game of life real? Is life a continuous circle, a cycle of reincarnation, that returns to itself in ever-evolving levels of awareness leading to enlightenment? Do reincarnation and creating your own reality really work this way? What do you think?

FOUR

The Energy Expressions of Your Experiences

The energy expressions of your experiences are the ways that the many pieces of your experiences play out in the karmic situations and circumstances in your life, whether the karma originated in a past life or a future life, because of the energies of what occurred in the past or future situation that originated the karma. Your present life is influenced just as much by what you do or did in the future as by what you do or did in the past.

You create karma and energy expressions every day through what you do as you create your own reality in the present. You can look into the future to see the energy expressions of your present experiences as they now exist in the form of possibilities and probabilities in your future lives. A *possibility* is an experience that *may* occur. A *probability* is an experience that is *likely to* occur.

Looking into your future lives to see the possibilities and probabilities of what will happen to you is pretty much the same thing as looking into your past lives to see the karma you created that is playing out in the present, then looking into your present life to see your probable near future based on what is occurring now, and by what you're doing about it through your thoughts, feelings, actions, and reactions. The experiences you've had in the past, and your reactions to them, set the stage for the probable future that you're experiencing now. What you see in the present will set the stage for your karma to play out in a probable future life or later in this life.

What you see as a possibility or probability later in your present life or in a future life may very well change before it actually occurs. This is because your thoughts and feelings about it, and your interconnected, corresponding experiences and karma relative to it, will change the energy as it is in the process of manifesting. When you change anything—through your thoughts and feelings about it, and by your actions—in the past, present, or future, the energy expressions of your experiences change correspondingly. What exists in the realm of possibilities and probabilities is directed through your thoughts and feelings, and by how you focus the energies of those possibilities and probabilities through your actions.

HYPOTHETICAL HAPPENINGS

Let's look at some possibilities and probabilities of hypothetical happenings to see how they may play out. Let's say in a past life you were a real estate developer in the Old West who cheated other people out of their money. They gave you their money to buy land, packed up their families and all their belongings in a covered wagon, and drove out West, only to find that you had pocketed their money and skipped town. You've racked up some bad karma that has to be corrected. Your karma will play out in future energy expressions of your actions.

In the present, which is now your future life from your Old West past life, you're a broker on Wall Street, investing other people's money. This is a possible future based on the past. The career you're in now offers you the opportunity to either balance the energy of your karma by being honest or to rack up more bad points by cheating your clients, not investing their money in stocks but investing it in your pocket or lying to them about how their stocks are doing and pocketing the profits for yourself.

Another possible, more probable (and maybe a simultaneous) future is that you're a real estate agent or a land developer. This would be the most likely scenario, as it almost duplicates the circumstances in your past life, for the energy expressions to play out and for you to either balance your karma or make it worse. The karmic test would be whether you invested your client's money in the land or house they bought, or whether you pocketed their money and skipped town again.

Another probable future scenario, contained within the broker lifetime, for you to experience the karmic energy expressions of what you created in your past life, is that you're also a homeowner. You apply for a mortgage equity loan on your home because you're on the verge of going bankrupt and losing all the investment in your house. The banker (let's say he was one of the people you swindled in the Old West) said your loan was denied when it really wasn't and put the loan proceeds into his pocket to buy a condo out West. Now you've experienced the energy expressions of the karma you created.

The banker is also experiencing the energy expressions of his past karma playing out in the present. Because he was cheated out of his home in the Old West, he responds by cheating you out of your money and buys a home for himself in the West. But maybe, just maybe, because he cheated you out of the money that would allow you to keep your home, he created the energy expressions of his karma that played out by you swindling him out of his land in the Old West.

How do you respond to losing the money you needed to keep your home? There are several possible scenarios you can create for yourself to experience in one or more lifetimes. Let's say that you didn't lose your house because you cheated your stock clients out of their money. You didn't understand your karma, and you certainly didn't balance it. You've compounded it and made it worse. The present energy expressions of the Old West scenario gave you a golden opportunity to either balance your karma or make it worse. You need to experience being homeless in order to understand and balance your Old West karma.

In another probable future life, you're going to see the energy expressions of both the past life and your present life play out in a similar scenario. You're again going to be offered the opportunity to balance the original karma you created in the Old West and compounded when you were a broker. Let's say in a future life after your broker lifetime, you're dirt-poor and homeless. These are the energy expressions of your past-present experiences synchronizing themselves in your future situation and balancing themselves, seemingly with no effort on your part; you're just a helpless victim of your present circumstances (not!)—circumstances that you created in two past lifetimes. You become a farmer, living off the land and respecting the value of the land. You live in a crude hut that you've built yourself.

Another possible future scenario is that, after your farmer lifetime, you reincarnate as a millionaire with a chain of hotels in the West. Being rich and having a home is the payoff for the good karma you've earned by valuing land. Being a good-hearted person now in your future life because you were so poor in another life, you let homeless people stay in your hotel for free. Maybe these homeless people are the ones you swindled out of their land in the Old West.

Or maybe you revert back to the pattern of your bad habits. Maybe your future life happened before a past life and created the energy expressions of your experiences in the Old West. It's possible, even probable, that this future millionaire-hotel lifetime is where it all started. Maybe all those homeless people you were so nice to, the ones you gave a home to, ruined all your hotels and you ended up penniless, on the street, vowing to yourself that you'd get these people if it was the last thing you ever did because they cheated you out of your home. (This vow will create the energy expressions of experiences in another lifetime.)

Let's throw simultaneous time into the picture. All of these lifetimes are happening at the same time in different spaces of time and vibrations of energy. Each experience influences all the other related experiences, and every choice made in every lifetime is reflected in all the interrelated experiences.

Look at an overall picture to see how it all works when it's happening simultaneously. Your hotel and the Old West lifetimes are happening concurrently in what only appears to be two different lifetimes, along with the farmer and broker lifetimes. When you let the homeless people stay in your hotel, providing them a home, you were—at the same time—trying to provide land and a home to the settlers who were coming out West.

When the homeless people wrecked your hotels, you lost everything. When the banker foreclosed on your home, you lost everything. Your farmer lifetime is still fresh in your mind because you're so poor, and because it's happening concurrently. You don't want to have to go back to being homeless and living off the land again—that was a really hard lifetime that you'd rather not repeat. (This strong feeling will cause you to experience being poor again—that's the energy expression of your feeling that will play out in another lifetime until you change that feeling.) Your combined feelings about being poor, and your reactions to losing your chain of hotels and your home, are a pivotal experience that created the attitude and actions you took in the Old West in response to what occurred when the homeless people wrecked your hotels.

Look at the vow you made—that you would get these people and make them pay. When your soul recognized that the Old West people were the same souls as the homeless people, you seized the opportunity to make them pay. You forgot what you had learned about the value of land in your farmer lifetime due to your feelings about being poor and having to struggle, and because of what you experienced when you lost your home in the broker lifetime. You cheated those souls out of their land just as they cheated you out of your chain of hotels and your home. This cycle will continue revolving and returning in circles of possible and probable pasts, presents, and futures until the energy expressions of the karma are balanced. Once balanced, the energy will move in another direction.

Let's not forget the land developer/real estate agent lifetime. After experiencing all the above lifetimes simultaneously, you reincarnate into what you think is your present life, in which you become a real estate agent to provide yourself with a perfect opportunity for you to balance all the negative energy expressions of several other lifetimes. What do you do now in the present, and how will it affect the experiences in what you think are the past and the future? The possibilities can get rather infinite; there are so many variances and influences that affect the energy and cause it to change. That's all part of the big picture.

REAL-LIFE SITUATIONS AND SCENARIOS

Your present experiences are linked to karma, either good or bad, that you've created in your past and future lives. One of my clients, Carol, was having problems with her husband, Jim. They were contemplating divorce because he was seeing another woman. Carol wanted to stay together and work things out, even though her husband no longer had a romantic interest in her. In a past-life regression, she became aware of a past life in which they were also married. She had cheated on him because the romance had gone out of their relationship. In that life, she left him to be with her lover.

In this life, the roles are reversed. She's going through the energy expressions of the karma she created. She's experiencing what she did to someone else; she's feeling what it's like to be cheated on. She wants to stay together in this life to balance what seems to be the bad karma between them. Her husband wants to leave to marry the other woman.

During the session, I instructed her to go into another lifetime in which they would be together again. I asked what the relationship was, and if there were any problems with it. She said she was in a future life, that they were brothers, and that they were very close. I asked her to immerse herself in the feelings she felt for her future brother and to bring those feelings into her present relationship, to surround it with the closeness she felt for her future brother who is now her present husband. As she brought the future feelings into the present, she was able to forgive her husband for cheating and was also able to forgive herself for what she had done before.

I asked her to notice that the karma between them had apparently been balanced because in a future life, they were together with a strong connection between them, though it wasn't a romantic one. I then guided her into the near future in this life and asked what was happening with her husband. She said they had stayed together (a probable present future), and it felt as if they were brother and sister. Her husband continued to see the other woman.

I instructed her to return again to the future life, in which they were brothers, to gather more information. She saw that the woman her present husband was seeing now was her future brother's wife. She became aware of the great love her present husband/future brother had for that woman. She realized that she and her present husband were not meant to be together and that their romantic relationship had created conflict within their souls. Because she had a great brotherly love for her present husband in the future, she wanted him to be happy, both in the present and in the future.

After the regression, we talked about whether she would stay with her husband in a platonic relationship (the probable present future she had seen or hoped for), or if she would let the relationship go. By looking into the future and seeing that their relationship as brothers was the one they were both happiest in, she was able to let her husband go in this life with feelings of love, knowing that their souls were together again in the future in a brotherly love relationship. Due to her actions in the present of letting her husband go, she created the probable future for them to experience as brothers. It's important to note that she balanced her karma in the present by letting go of the relationship in a positive way.

If she had let it go with feelings of anger, those angry feelings would have showed up in a future life as energy expressions of unresolved emotions.

Karma continues from lifetime to lifetime. Karma isn't etched in stone. It is constantly changing with the choices and decisions you make, and with your attitude and actions—past, present, and future. These go in many various possible and probable directions as their energy expressions appear in your experiences.

For example, and to oversimplify matters, here's another hypothetical happening. You decide to call in sick to work. You've done this several times before. This choice gets you the day off, but there may be various repercussions due to the energy you've created and put into motion with this decision. Your boss may or may not believe that you're really sick and could do one of several possible things. He or she may believe you and be concerned about you, and tell you to feel better. Or he or she could make you get a doctor's note before you return to work, write you up with a warning, or fire you. What your boss does in relation to what you've done is to react to the energy that you've set in motion. It's possible that you won't get fired if you've only called in a few times, but if calling in sick is a regular habit, there is a good probability of you losing your job. All choices and decisions have consequences in the form of the energy expressions of your experiences.

If goofing off or not wanting to go to work because you'd rather be doing something else that you think is more important, is a soul pattern that plays out in the present, it could have been created in the past in a lazy lifetime, and you carried over this karmic tendency into your present life. That's one probable karmic scenario in past-present terms as it plays out in the present-future.

Look at this a bit differently, in reverse. In a future life, you had difficulty finding and/or keeping a job. That's the energy expressions of being lazy in a past life playing out. The future life created your karmic present, which then reverberated into a past life.

Because of this future life in which you can't find or keep a job, you assume the attitude that work isn't important, so you call in sick to work in the present, and become lazy about work in the past.

Consider two more things in this scenario: All these past-present-future lives are happening simultaneously, each influencing and affecting the other. It's probable that, in either a past or a future lifetime, or possibly in the present, your karma will be to learn responsibility and the value of work. It's also possible that you're not doing the work you're meant to be doing—the purpose your soul set out for you to achieve in this life—and this causes the tendency to call in sick to work so you can pursue your soul's purpose, which you think is more important.

Your future and past experiences hold the consequences of and mirror the choices and decisions you make now and for who you are now. Who you are now and what you do will be reflected in the future and the past as either a possibility or a probability. It may reflect a turnaround of who you are now and what you're doing, or it may be almost identical.

Karma, whether it was created in the past or the future, has to be balanced. One of my clients, Chris, was having a lot of difficulties with her sister. They were both very competitive and argued constantly, each trying to best the other. Chris was tired of the constant bickering and wanted to have peace between them. She came for a past-life regression to see where the rivalry started; she wanted to understand it better so she could resolve it. I directed her to go to the lifetime in which this problem began. Instead of going into the past, as she had expected, she arrived in the future in which both she and her sister worked as scientists in a highly sophisticated think tank.

They were each trying to outdo the other, not sharing the results of their research and experiments to further the project they were working on together; and this created the pattern for the intense rivalry they felt now. I suggested that she combine forces with her sister in the future lifetime, so she could create peace between them that would also carry over into a peaceful present. In her future life, she talked to her sister and offered to share information with her. She told her sister that there was no need for the competition; that if they worked together, they could do so much more than if they were on opposing sides. They agreed to combine their knowledge to come up with bigger and better results.

You can look at this in several ways. Perhaps the present competitiveness created a similar pattern in the future, or maybe the future showed Chris what would happen if the present problem continued and was not resolved. Or maybe the future influenced the present more than she thought. I saw her several months after the regression, and she told me that she and her sister had worked things out between them and were now enjoying a relaxed, noncompetitive relationship. By going into a future life, she was able to resolve a present problem when it began and to change the energy expressions of her present and future experiences.

In relation to your karma, instead of things seeming to happen to you out of the clear blue sky, wouldn't it be great to see the possible and probable energy expressions of your experiences and change them before they occurred, if you didn't like the way the picture was playing out? What if you could balance your karma before it happened? Then there would be no need to carry it over into a future life, where it would surface as a bit of a surprise because you wouldn't know where it was coming from.

MIND-EXPANDING MEDITATION: MULTIDIMENSIONAL MIRRORS

The past, present, and future are all mirrors of one another, reflecting transparent, see-through images. Your present experiences will show you reflections of the past and the future, and how their energy expressions are intricately interwoven into the same picture, superimposed both on and within the same space.

As you become aware of the way your present experiences mirror your past and future experiences, you'll see reflections of the interrelated experiences in your past and future lives in the present. You can look into a multidimensional mirror within your mind to see the reflections of all the possibilities and probabilities of the energy expressions of your experiences based on who you are now and what you're doing.

A multidimensional mirror is like a kaleidoscope. A kaleidoscope is a cylinder with mirrors and colored shapes inside that, when rotated, creates shifting symmetrical patterns. It shows a complex, colorful, shifting pattern or scene, reflecting a complex set of events or circumstances. A kaleidoscope shows myriad images. Turn it just a fraction and a completely new image appears, but it's the same elements viewed in a slightly different manner. It's the same with your perceptions and perspectives of the experiences in your past, present, and future lives. A change of perspective, a shift of perception, and a whole new picture—in infinite variations—of possibilities and probabilities appears.

As you look through the kaleidoscope of your experiences— through the multidimensional spaces of time—you'll see all the resplendent, colorful pictures of past-present-future possibilities and probabilities of the energy expressions of your experiences vibrating in shifting symmetrical patterns.

In your inner awareness, your mind's eye, imagine that you have a magical, multidimensional mirror you can look into that will transport you anywhere in time to show you multifaceted reflections and pictures of your past-present-future experiences as you are in the process of creating them and as they are simultaneously in the process of playing out.

In addition to looking at the reflection of your present thoughts, feelings, actions, and reactions to see into the near future in this lifetime, and looking into your mind's mirror to review enhanced images of scenes in your past lives or to preview events in your future lives, you can look into and through the kaleidoscopic multidimensional mirror of time to see the reflection of all your experiences in all your past-present-future lives as they are happening and as they simultaneously interact with and influence one another. You can see the effect of what you set into motion through your thoughts, feelings, choices, decisions, and actions in this life.

This multidimensional mirror of time that reflects the energy expressions of your experiences shows all your possible and probable past, present, and future experiences simultaneously. Your experiences, thoughts, emotions, imagination, and your inner awareness are your mirror into seeing through the vibrations of time that can take you back to the future, forward into the past, and show you the present in a new way by looking within your mind.

Bend your thoughts around the present. Look at your present experiences from a different thought perspective, from an altered image perception. Shift your frame of mind; see things differently from the way you are used to observing them. As a reference point, think about an experience in your present life that you want to see all the many possible and probable energy expressions of in your past and future lives, as well as looking at the reflections that are mirrored in the past and future in the present. View a situation in which you want to see how the karma will play out, and what caused and created the karma in the first place. Focus your frame of awareness and point of view to fit the reflections as they show themselves.

Watch the kaleidoscope of your past and future experiences mirrored and reflected in your present experiences. See through the reflections to understand the images of future experiences that are mirrored in your life now and reflected in the past, and past experiences that are mirrored in your life now and reflected in the future. Within your mind, watch the changing energies in motion as your experiences show themselves in all their shifting, symmetrical patterns and expressions.

See how things may play out and what may come into being as several possibilities and probabilities, based on your thoughts and feelings, on what is occurring now, and what you're doing about it. Shift your perspective and perception; watch how the images change. Make choices and changes based on what you see, so that you are reflecting the energies of symmetrical, simultaneous choices and changes into your future, present, and past lives to see the full range of their energy expressions.

There are myriad energy expressions that can come about from your thoughts, feelings, actions, and choices as you see them in the future, present, and past. Look into your multidimensional mirror of time that shows you all the reflections of the experiences in your past-present-future lives simultaneously to see all the kaleidoscopic possibilities and probabilities to determine what you want to do in the present and to see how what you do now will affect the energy expressions of your experiences in past and future lives.

Play with the possibilities and probabilities you see by making choices and changes. When you've made a choice or a change, put that energy into motion to explore and experience the energy expressions—the possibilities and probabilities—that your choice and actions will bring about in your past-present-future lives. Cause, change, create, un-create, re-create, and rearrange the energy vibrations of your past-present-future experiences to see all their possible and probable energy expressions. Go with the flow of your thoughts and feelings and what you see in your multidimensional mirror images.

The choices and decisions you make now and put into action will be reflected in your past and future lives as energy expressions of your present experiences, just as the actions you've taken and the choices you've made in other lives created the energy expressions of your present experiences.

If the simultaneous time-space concept is a bit too much for you to wrap your mind around just yet, and if your multidimensional mirror images were a bit blurry or out of focus, you can still expand your mind beyond the boundary of physical time and space by looking at one thing at a time in the present to see what the energy expressions of your karma are, to see what the future—in this life and in your future lives—holds for you. You can look into the future to see what's in store for you, based on present choices and decisions, by seeing how your present experiences reflect similar past and future experiences.

UNSEEN ENERGIES

However, don't get too comfortable looking at only one thing at a time. The various choices and changes you make in your life every day as you create your own reality through your thought perspectives and image perceptions—through the way you think your thoughts and the way you see your experiences—create myriad possible and probable experiences. Tracing the energy vibrations of your experiences in the present to see your future in this lifetime will show you how to trace the energies into seeing events in your future lives. The energies of possible and probable experiences follow the energy of your thoughts, feelings, and actions. There are millions of ways that this energy can go. By making various choices and changes, which you do every day about everything in your life, you're creating your future reality, both in this life and in future lives.

Every choice you make happens somewhere, sometime. Every word, thought, feeling, idea, intent, and action—being composed of energy—manifests into matter in direct proportion to the energy you put into it. While you may be aware of only the immediate, physical consequences of your thoughts or actions, once you've put your choices into motion, just by thinking, feeling, or acting on them, they will reappear in your life in some form as karma.

Every time you change your mind, you change your reality; you alter the direction of your life and you change the direction of the energy expressions of your experiences. When you change the energies of a past or future experience in the present, you automatically create another energy expression of your experience. Energy doesn't ever disappear; it reappears in new forms, some seen through the visible effects of your experiences and some unseen through the invisible energies of your thoughts and feelings. These energies interact with, and permeate every part of your past, present, and future lives. You can place your awareness into these unseen energies in the present, the future, and the past by looking within your mind and your feelings.

Your feelings are very powerful, more powerful than thoughts or actions. For example, think about a special person in your life. How long have you loved him or her? How long do you think you'll love this person? Forever? Are your feelings today the same as they were yesterday? Will you love him or her more tomorrow? Or will the love you feel for this person change direction and turn into something else? Will love turn into friendship or fade away altogether, or will it turn into contempt, disgust, or hate? Once it goes in that direction, will it return to love? Emotions are energy. As your emotions change, so does the energy surrounding your emotions as it affects the experiences that your feelings are intertwined with while changing the energy expressions.

For another example, how long can you hold a grudge? A day? A week? A month? A year? A lifetime? Forever? Until that person somehow redeems him- or herself? A grudge is an emotion and is filled with energy. Look at your thoughts and feelings to see where their energy expressions go. Perhaps you've said things such as, "This person gives me a headache," or "I'm really upset by this situation." Later, maybe that same day, you had a headache or your stomach hurt for no apparent reason. Maybe your thoughts and feelings, composed of energy, came back to bite you.

While you may have forgotten thoughts you've had or feelings you've expressed or words you've said with strong emotions attached, such as love or hate, anger or compassion, those words and thoughts, along with the energy of their intertwined feelings, have been created by you and their energy expressions will continue, returning to you in your present life or appearing in another life in which they will affect you.

You also create various energy expressions when you think about the future, about what you'd like to do and the things you'd like to have happen. You're creating your own reality as you're looking into the future; you're creating a multitude of possibilities and probabilities through your thoughts, feelings, beliefs, and actions. Depending on the energy you put into those thoughts, feelings, and actions—and your beliefs about them—those experiences will occur in one form or another, at some point and place in time.

The energy expressions of a *possible* experience exist and wait for you to experience them simply because you've thought of the possible experience once or twice. A *probable* experience is much more likely to occur, because you've given it much more thought and consideration—you've put more of your feelings into it and given it more energy to exist. However, the possible experience that you thought about once or twice will manifest in direct proportion to the energy you've given it. Every thought, feeling, and action manifests somewhere, sometime as an energy expression in your experiences.

FIVE

The Motions of Matter

Before we get into the motions of matter, let's talk about reality
and illusion as they pertain to the energy of existence and the
creation of experiences and circumstances in relationship to
time. Time and the physical matter of your experiences are very
intricate and interwoven vibrations of energy; they pattern and
weave the tapestry of your thoughts, feelings, beliefs, and actions
into the expressions of all your experiences. The energy threads of
your experiences shape and form into physical matter in the present
as they simultaneously move through the motions of matter in
other lifetimes.

Your perceptions form your reality. How does time fit into your
concept of reality? On a linear level, the past is history, the present
is occurring now, and the future hasn't happened yet. Time is
measured by the moving forward of moments. This serves as an
orderly, logical framework of time, but is true only on a physical
level. Toss thought energy and spiritual reality into the picture,
and things change dramatically.

You might wonder why we're not consciously aware of all the
past and future parts of our present experiences. Because we're in

physical form, we've limited our awareness to focusing only on the present physical energies of space and time and how they appear in our three-dimensional Earth reality. This present time, this physical space, this Earth dimension, this physical vibration of energy, is what we choose to be aware of now. This is where we've placed our awareness, where we've focused our attention and directed our thoughts. What would we see and become aware of if we changed our focus of awareness to encompass the true reality of our spirit?

While you're thinking about that, think about this: What if time is an illusion? What if time exists relevant to your involvement with it and your thoughts and beliefs about it? What if time exists in various levels of energy, in different frameworks of awareness, and you're more or less aware of it at different times or at different levels of awareness, depending on your perception and belief?

How do you differentiate between reality and illusion? What's real for you, and what makes it real? If you believe that something exists, then it does. If you believe that something doesn't exist, then it doesn't. If the person sitting next to you believes that something exists, no matter what that person says or does, if you don't believe it, then it doesn't exist for you. This is where illusion comes into the picture.

For example, let's talk religion for a moment. Many people believe in God, but some don't. If God is real to you, but not to someone else, does God exist? Yes and no. God exists for you, but not for the atheist sitting next to you. We've got something that exists and is real for one person, but that doesn't exist and is an illusion for another person. How can that be? How can something exist and not exist at the same time? How can reality and illusion coexist?

Before you answer that, let's look at what you perceive your physical reality to be. Maybe your reality does or doesn't exist. Maybe it's real; maybe it's an illusion. For example, in the North, winter is cold, snowy, and gray; but for people who live in the

South, winter is warm and sunny. What reality is real? The one you're experiencing and the one you're involved in? On any given day in the North during the winter, it can be 30 degrees below zero Fahrenheit, and it can be 80 degrees above zero somewhere in the South at exactly the same time.

Just because you're walking through the snow and shivering, and someone else, at the same time, is swimming at a warm, sunny beach, does that mean his or her reality doesn't exist because you're not experiencing it? If both realities exist, and they do, but one is more real to you because you're experiencing it and you're involved with it, then doesn't it depend on where you focus your awareness? Let me ask you again. What would you see and be aware of if you focused your awareness into your spiritual reality rather than just your physical reality?

Now that you may be half-thinking that your physical reality doesn't exist, let's go back a few paragraphs to the thought, What if time is an illusion, just as your physical reality may be an illusion? What if someone who was playing a huge practical cosmic joke on us, "invented" time to run our lives in a logical, orderly, and rhythmic manner? What if the real nature of time has been squished and warped into limited, linear expressions of its many multidimensional forms and vibrations to fit into a three-dimensional Earth reality?

When we see beyond our limited physical awareness into our spiritual reality, we see the true nature of time for what it really is, and we're aware of ourselves living in the past, the present, and the future at the same time. This fits in perfectly with the simultaneous time-space concept that everything in the past and the future occurs in the present in different vibrations of energy at varying frequencies of motion in harmony with space and matter.

Think of time as energy. Like energy, time is, was, and always will be. Time can be directed, focused, and transmuted (changed) by your thoughts, feelings, and beliefs, and through your perspectives and perceptions. Seeing through the illusion of physical time into the energies of your experiences shows you that time, in a physical framework, is really an illusion. In a spiritual framework, your soul creates your Earth experiences in and through the multidimensional energies of time. While you are on Earth in the three-dimensional world, you have free will to choose what you want to do about your karma through your thoughts and feelings, which result in the actions you take in your experiences.

When you put your thoughts and feelings in motion through the act of thinking a thought or feeling an emotion, the energy of matter—the energy expressions of your experiences—begins to form into the shape of your experiences in space and time, and your thoughts and feelings begin to show themselves as visible vibrations of energy in the matter of your experiences. This is how time vibrates and how matter is put into motion in the physical and spiritual realms to create situations and circumstances from your present thoughts and feelings and from other experiences in past and future lives.

Let's put physical matter into the picture and look into and through the spaces of time. When something exists in the present, it can be physically seen and touched. When that same thing exists in the same place, but either in the past or in the future, it can no longer be physically seen or touched, yet it's still there because it exists in another vibration of time, in another level of energy.

For example, in *The Time Machine*, by H. G. Wells, the time machine stayed in the same place; but, as time moved forward and backward, the time machine could no longer be seen. It still occupied the same space, but had "moved" into another vibration of time. Actually, it didn't move at all. It was still there in the same space, but in a different vibration of energy. This brings up an interesting question of how we determine what is actually real and how we perceive our reality. Is something real only if we can detect it in a physical manner?

Depending on how you perceive time as it shows itself in your present life, and your beliefs about your experiences relative to the spiritual influence of energies in past, present, and future events, you can work with the energies of time to create, re-create, or un-create past, present, and future events both before they occur and after they happen. You can rearrange and change the motions of energy into matter. You can shape your experiences so that they are the way you'd like them to be.

Changing the past in a linear manner changes the present as you know it now and also affects and changes the future. The vibrations of time and energy are malleable; they can be shaped and reshaped. The energies of past events aren't inactive; they're still very active and can be changed in the present. When you change the energies of past events, you simultaneously change the corresponding interwoven energies of the present and the future as they relate to that changed event.

You can go into the past and create or change the energies of an event to shape your present and support your future. By doing this, it will affect your present and future. You can change the future to reshape your past. If you go into the future to create an event, you also need to go into either the present or the past to create the support or background for that event. You need to pull together the threads of energy for the event to exist as matter in your physical reality. However, considering the simultaneous time-space concept, the past-present energy is already there because of the interwoven future vibrations that created the framework for it to exist in your reality.

Physical time appears to be an illusion; it becomes real through your perceptions of it and your beliefs about it. In a linear manner, everything you're doing now, in your current reality, is supported by your past, experienced in your present, and is building the foundation for your future. In a spiritual manner, time flows through the vibrational spaces of the past, present, and future simultaneously, creating, supporting, shaping, and building your experiences in all your past-present-future lives.

Time, space, and the motions of matter in your physical reality can be transcended and transmuted on a spiritual thought-energy level. Time, space, and matter then become uncharacteristic of your physical reality. When you transcend time, you're actually transmuting the energies of it. One immediate physical benefit is that you can consciously transcend time to help you determine what you want to do in your experiences and help you make choices based on the energy that would be directed if a certain choice were made—and put into motion through your thoughts and feelings and by your actions—or not made.

This will follow a stream of possibilities and probabilities. In order for something to exist, the possibility must be there in the first place. To become a probability, energy must be focused in that direction. You can transmute time to explore and experience all the possibilities and probabilities of any given situation. You can see how your choices will manifest or would have manifested if you had done things differently. Depending on how you perceive time, and the way you transcend time, you can create, shape, mold, change, and/or un-create past, present, and future events.

Keep in mind, though, that all your actions, and each and every experience, emotion, thought, and idea you have—in all of your past, present, and future lives—interact with and influence every related aspect in all your lives at the same time. This is because everything is composed of energy. Anything you change in the present, for example, will similarly affect and change corresponding things in both the past and the future.

In creating and changing the energy vibrations of events, remember that energy is malleable and can be changed according to your beliefs and desires. The energy you change, and the way you change it, will cause karma—cause and effect—to come into play. There are repercussions and consequences to everything you do. The energy will reverberate and ripple through all the interrelated experiences that are connected to the changed situation.

If you go into the past and change, create, or un-create an event, it will affect the energies of related events in your present and your future. If you go into the future to change, create, or un-create an event, you also need to go into the present or the past to create the support for that event or to become aware of the energy that already exists there and to mold it into the shape of what you want it to be.

In a spiritual framework of reality, you change, create, and un-create events in all three energy levels of time—past, present, and future—simultaneously, because this is how energy works. (You'll see and experience how this works in the mind-opening meditation in the next chapter.) Transmuting time as it expresses itself on a physical level is only one aspect. You change time and the energy of events as they shape and form into the motions of matter in the past, present, and future simultaneously, whether you're aware of it or not.

Transmuting time is the same thing as changing your perception of time. Within your spiritual awareness, you can transmute and transcend time, space, and matter. Remember that time is an expression of energy. Where you place time (in the past, present, or future), and how you perceive time (through your thoughts and beliefs), will determine how you perceive and experience the energy manifesting. However, regardless of your perceptions and beliefs, the energies of time will manifest and express themselves in all three levels of the past, present, and future simultaneously, because this is the true nature of time.

You can transcend time and change events that have already occurred. When you do this, the changes you make are reflected in your current experiences. All the energy vibrations of your experiences exist here and now in the present, even when they seem to be happening in the past or the future. The repercussions and echoes of energy affect and alter what appear to be past and future experiences in present choices. Once a choice has been made, all the energies related to that choice re-vibrate and change accordingly. This is how the past can be changed—by rearranging the energies of your thoughts and feelings in the present.

I once heard a wonderful story about how someone changed a fear in the present by going into the past and changing the past event that originated the fear. A perfectly nice gentleman was thrown off a bridge by some not-so-nice people just because he was in the wrong place at the wrong time. Of course, he died; and when he was reincarnated into his present life, he was born with an overwhelming fear of bridges. He didn't know why he was terrified of them.

As an adult, he would avoid bridges at all costs. This got to be a little troublesome because he couldn't travel very far without encountering one. Every time he came to a bridge, he would have to turn back or detour to find a way around it. He went to see a hypnotherapist, who regressed him to find the origin of his fear. This nice gentleman tripped into the past life in which he was thrown off a bridge and relived his death scene.

The hypnotherapist suggested that he view being thrown off the bridge in a different manner. She suggested that instead of being thrown off a bridge, he could pick some flowers that were close by, then walk onto the bridge, and throw the flowers off it. As the not-so-nice people came up to him to throw him off the bridge, the gentleman turned around and gave them flowers, and they left him alone.

The point of this story is that the gentleman is no longer afraid of bridges. Now he likes bridges. He changed his perceived outcome of the situation, and it also changed his fear. He reshaped the matter and energies of his past experience. In changing his perception, he changed the energy vibrations of the past event. That changed energy then rippled and reverberated through his present and carried forward into his future.

INTERACTIVE EXPERIENCE: TURNING BACK THE HANDS OF TIME

You can change the outcome of any event in the past by changing your feelings about it and your perceptions of it in the present so that the expressions of your past and present experience are different. What exists now as a past experience is one expression of energy; you can change that energy to create, re-create, or un-create an event and experience a new past. You can change what actually occurred in your past lives.

Think about a past event, either in this life or in a past life that you're aware of, that you'd like to change. It doesn't have to be a fear of bridges. It can be something you wish you hadn't done or an experience you wish hadn't happened to you. Think about why you'd like to change it and how you'd rearrange something that has already occurred.

Return, in your mind, to an important event in this lifetime, or in a past life, that you'd like to change. See the images and emotions of the event projected onto a movie screen in your mind's eye so that you can see it in colorful, moving images, hear the sounds of it, and feel every detail as you simultaneously watch yourself participate in the event. Clearly focus on your present emotions about it; center in on your feelings about why you want to change the past event. This is the energy you'll be working with. Project the event, along with your feelings, into the picture on the screen in your mind.

Watch all the various aspects of your past event play out. You have an increased understanding of how and why it occurred and why you responded the way you did then. Remember and reexperience the part you played in this event. Remember and reexperience your thoughts and feelings, actions, and reactions, as you watch them on the screen.

Time doesn't exist. This event is happening for the first time. It's no longer a memory. It's real and is happening right now. Be inside this event. Be completely there in heart, mind, and soul as you watch yourself experiencing this event.

You're free to change your feelings about this event as you're involved in it. You're free to change your attitude and your emotions, your thoughts, your feelings, and your actions as you're watching yourself participate in it. You're free to rewrite and re-script this event in any way that you want. You're free to change the outcome of this event by changing your feelings and your reactions to it and by changing and rearranging what actually occurred.

You're free to change the part you played in this event, thereby changing the outcome, and changing the outcome for anyone else who is involved. You can change and rearrange the energy of this event so that it plays out in the way you desire in both the past and the present. As you change your perception of and attitude about this event, the energy of the event itself is changed. The changed energy also influences anyone else who was involved, because the vibrations of your attitude and perception, which are composed of thought energies, influence and affect other people.

As you change, rearrange, and reshape the energy of the past, it flows into the present; and you're now aware of this past event in a new frame of awareness. Watch how your changed feelings about the event, and the event itself, show themselves on your movie screen as you watch yourself experiencing your changed past reality. Bring the energies of the changed past event and your feelings about it into your present. See how it affects you now and what your thoughts and feelings are about it. It is now a "new" past event that influences and interacts with your present, as it simultaneously affects and influences the future energies connected with it.

Because you've traveled backward through time and changed the energies of a past event to see how it shows itself in your present, you know you can also travel forward in time. This is a two-part movie that continues in the next chapter. Watch your movie screen to see the preview of coming attractions. From your present perception of this event, watch how you travel its changed energies into the future to see how the changes you made in the past now appear in the future. But don't become too attached to what you see or what you think may occur based on past-present energies; we'll be throwing a lot of other things into the picture simultaneously.

That was a nice linear trip that leaned into the future a little bit. Well, it did more than lean; it led you into interrelated future energies to see how they occur from a past-present frame of time. In the next chapter, you'll be viewing this movie screen again, but a bit differently, as you change what hasn't happened yet in the future to correspond with your present and your past.

Simultaneous Time, Space, and Synchronicity

Your future lives are happening now in simultaneous spaces, in synchronicity with your past lives and present life in a circular flow of time. The present is your pivot point into seeing both the past and the future simultaneously, because the past, the present, and the future are all happening in the same time span of here and now.

I read an article about retroactive prayer which shows that past and future time vibrate together in the present, whether the event seems to happen in the past or the future. In a scientific study, the ten-year-old hospital records of 10,000 patients with heart disease were looked at. Half of them were prayed for; the other half were not. When the records were checked, it was discovered that the group that was prayed for healed faster and the healing was more complete, even though these patients were prayed for ten years after being discharged from the hospital. The time they were being prayed for was happening simultaneously with the time they were in the hospital even though the time of the prayers actually occurred ten years in the future in linear time. The future prayers were beneficial in the past because the past and the future are both contained within the present—within the eternal now.

The seemingly separate realities of past, present, and future that we live in simultaneously (this is not a paradox or an oxymoron, even though it seems to be) constantly interact with and influence each other through the energy vibrations of time. Luminous light threads of your thoughts, feelings, and actions connect the energy vibrations of past, present, and future experiences together, as they weave a picture of all the experiences in your life.

Life is energy in motion; all your thoughts, feelings, and experiences are relative to one another and are influenced by interweaving, interrelated vibrations of energy. The energies of your experiences express themselves on many levels concurrently. Everything is happening simultaneously in time and space at various vibrations of energy in different rates of motion that are vibrating in harmony with each other. Experiences and events in your past, present, and future lives vibrate at the same time, but at different rates of energy.

Time is a vibration of energy; space is a dimension of motion. Both time and space are synchronized, vibrating in harmony. Because time is simultaneous, you can experience the past and the future in the present by synchronizing your complete awareness with your experiences. You can understand all the expressions of past and future experiences when you relate them to present experiences by centering in and focusing on what is happening in the present.

Your perceptions will influence the way your experiences appear to you in time. If you believe in the past, present, and future, then time will show itself in that illusion, though you'll often see divergences to your beliefs. This occurs because the way you see time and how you believe it happens in your reality—your perceptions—can limit your view of the real properties and qualities of time. The energies of time will show themselves in their true form regardless of your beliefs, though you may not see all the expressions of time energies.

The true nature of time is a circular, flowing rhythm of motion, showing itself in synchronicity with the matter of your experiences. Everything happens simultaneously in vibratory rates and forms of energy. If you try to capture or change the expression of time to fit your frame of thought and focus of awareness, it doesn't in any way, shape, form, or fashion change the real nature of time; it only changes the way you experience time. The same is true for experiences. When you place them in a limited, linear framework, and view them as happening separately in your past, present, and future lives, you're not able to see the true reality of your experiences—which are always happening simultaneously—because you've limited your perception of them.

When you place your thoughts into and synchronize your awareness with the simultaneous vibrations of your experiences, you'll be able to see all their energy expressions in your past, present, and future lives. Synchronous and simultaneous time, space, motion, and matter all work together in perfect harmony. The key to seeing all aspects of your past and future experiences is to see them in the framework of reference points, to associate them with interconnected experiences in your present life. You do this by centering in and focusing on the main event or emotion, which is the pivot point, to see all the interweaving, interrelated threads in simultaneous vibrations of time. Your awareness of your experiences—your past, present, and future memories—is triggered by association. Connecting with associated experiences and feelings, which are the interweaving light threads of energy, is what makes it so easy to remember events and emotions in past and future lives.

When an experience occurs in the present, its expressions also occur at the same time in perfect synchronicity with the energies of the original experience, whether the original experience occurred in the past, present, or future, while the expressions reverberate and ripple through the past, present, and future. Everything is happening at the same time in perfect synchronicity with vibrations and expressions of energy. A synonym for syn-chronicity is *timing*.

A dictionary definition of *synchronicity* is: "a coincidence of events that seem related; the coincidence of events that seem related but are not obviously caused one by the other." This seems to say that it's not obvious how one causes the other—but it's very obvious if you're tuned in to spiritual energy. This definition con-tinues: "an occurrence at the same time; the simultaneous occur-rence of two or more things; related items/situations that are coming together and happening at the same time." Actually, there's no such thing as coincidence. It's more like perfect timing—synchronicity.

In other words, synchronicity is two or more things happening at the same time that appear in the form of a coincidence or a chance encounter. It's the timing of events that happen simulta-neously, but seemingly independently of each other, and it appears as if they were planned by some means to bring about a certain event. You bet they were planned. You planned them before you were born into this life.

Your soul completely understands the nature of synchronicity and uses it to bring about certain experiences, sometimes through chances and coincidences, into your life. For example, when people synchronize their watches, they do so because they've agreed to do something at exactly the same moment in time. When you're choosing to reincarnate and you want to set up expe-riences with other souls, you synchronize your timing on the Earth plane in order to have those experiences and to either enhance your good karma or balance your bad karma.

Time flows in a circular motion, interweaving through all your experiences. The vibrations of time are in sync with each other and are connected through the harmony, or similarity of the asso-ciated events or emotions, in your experiences. When you center your attention into whatever you're thinking, feeling, doing, or experiencing at any given moment, the energies of time and its properties of space, matter, and motion blend together to become a fluid dimension of energy that flows in, around, and through your experiences, bringing past, present, and future together.

You blend the properties of time into vibrations of energy by relating them to a particular experience. When an experience is similar to or reminiscent of another experience, time becomes connected at a revolving point of energy when you synchronize your thoughts and feelings with that experience—when you focus your awareness into that experience. Your experience is timeless and exists simultaneously in related vibrational energies of the past, present, and future that are interwoven and in tune with each other. You can understand simultaneous time by looking at the events and emotions that occur in your present life by connecting them with similar feelings and experiences.

MIND-OPENING MEDITATION: TAPESTRY OF LIFE

You can feel the interwoven vibrations of time and see the many interrelated aspects of all your past, present, and future experiences by getting into the vibe of simultaneous time and synchronizing your awareness with it. You do this by centering your awareness into your mind—your soul—and focusing on the threads that connect the energies of your experiences together. You can bring your seemingly separate realities together by seeing how time is woven through the energy threads of your experiences.

Your life is like a tapestry that is in the process of being woven with luminous light threads of energy. Each thread interconnects and interweaves with all the other threads to form a complete picture of your past, present, and future lives in motion, with many colorful images of your soul patterns and your experiences woven in and through the design. The threads are interwoven with the experiences in your life, merging the physical and spiritual worlds. The threads of energy are continuously flowing through the tapestry of your experiences as they simultaneously weave the images together.

As you study the images, the tapestry becomes timeless, showing scenes from the past, present, and future, bringing them together and blending them into the ever-present here and now. Sometimes the images are still as you reflect upon them because the energy is not currently in motion. Other times, the images move in rhythm and harmony with the vibrations of your experiences, with the energies of your thoughts, feelings, and actions. Events are happening and changing all the time, pictures appearing and disappearing, yet the design always remains interrelated and connected.

Sometimes the images become superimposed upon one another, each image influencing and interacting with the thoughts and feelings that originally created and shared in shaping it. You see that all the images of your experiences are connected through vibrations of your thoughts, feelings, and actions; and that each image is synchronized in a perfect rhythm of movement with all the other images in the picture.

The luminescent light threads of energy weave in and out, around and through, and between the tapestry of your experiences as they unravel and weave together, curling and connecting to create and form new pictures while the original picture is in the process of shaping itself. The energy is in perpetual motion, in an ever-changing process of creation and expression, renewing and reshaping itself in every moment. Sometimes the images blur together, occurring simultaneously. Sometimes they appear as silhouettes, echoing one another. At other times, they run side by side, paralleling and mirroring each other. Sometimes the parallels merge; sometimes they go entirely different ways.

The picture moves in tune with your here and now thoughts and feelings, with the energies of your actions, the threads of light flowing and expanding into all your past-present-future experiences at once. You see how each of your actions causes reactions, and how those reactions create a chain of events and experiences that link together and weave through one another. At the same time, you see how and why your thoughts, feelings, and actions are interwoven with the expressions of your experiences, and how they are intricately intertwined within the energy of the pictures of your experiences. Even as you watch the images of your experiences flow through the motions of matter in time and space, you see that each and every experience is somehow influenced by an even higher vibration of your soul energy that interacts with your physical thoughts, feelings, and actions.

At times, the tapestry appears to be breathing. Both the physical and spiritual images and their interconnected experiences are alive with energy, vibrating and pulsating in a flowing, rhythmic movement, forming waves of energy that go everywhere at once, circling and spiraling into infinity.

The picture draws you within; you're inside the images and experiencing the scenes that the tapestry depicts. These events and emotions are the threads of your life, showing you the patterns of your soul and the pieces of your physical experiences that are intricately interwoven. As you go inside the images, you understand how and why each and every experience occurs, and you see the pattern of how your thoughts, feelings, and actions are woven into and through the fabric of your life.

Simultaneous time, space, and synchronicity work together in a timeless format. The energy of matter and motion vibrates inside your experiences to create chances and coincidences, and to shape and change the energies of past-present-future experiences. You can create new and different circumstances and situations, change previously existing experiences that have already happened while also changing events that have not yet occurred, by being in the vibe of simultaneous time—by getting into the rhythm and harmony of it, and by focusing and synchronizing your awareness and experiences with the energies of time.

Time, space, and matter are expressions of energy, vibrating at different rates. Time vibrates at rates of past, present, and future. Time also interacts and vibrates with matter in various dimensions of space. Time itself remains unchanged; it simply expresses itself through different vibrational rates of energy. The present seems to be happening separately here and now, even though it's perpetually created and simultaneously influencing your past and your future—just as those vibrations of time are constantly causing and creating the effects of what you experience by your present perceptions of feelings and your current perspectives of thoughts.

In a physical framework of matter, once an experience has occurred, it exists within that framework and is governed by physical laws, just as vibrations of that same experience exist on a spiritual level and are governed by spiritual laws. Your experience exists on both levels simultaneously in vibratory rates of past, present, and future; the levels affect and influence the energy vibrations of each other. This is how the energies of time vibrate in all your experiences and is the way that time flows through the spaces of your experiences to affect the motions and matter of them. You may have noticed this in the tapestry meditation earlier in this chapter.

You're aware of varying degrees of the influence, depending on your perceptions and the level of energy you're tuned in to. As you look into your experiences, you can see how they manifest in the vibrations of time, space, and matter through the motions of your thoughts, feelings, and actions. Look at the same experience in three different ways—from the past, present, and future—and on two levels of awareness—physical and spiritual—until you feel comfortable working with all levels of energy simultaneously.

Your experiences are meant to be looked at together—as a whole, not piecemeal or cut into past-present-future chunks. When you see all the energy expressions of your experiences simultaneously, you see the true reality of your experiences in all of their energy expressions.

Time doesn't move in a straight line; it moves in roundabout circles, returning to the same vibrations. As time vibrates, it ripples and repeats itself in related, similar experiences. Your experiences are a circular image of themselves with individual and synchronous characteristics and qualities, transcending time and always revolving and returning to the same interrelated energies. Time runs together, both before it occurs and after it happens, while it's in the process of revolving into past, present, and future experiences simultaneously. Time goes around in circles, repeating itself. Instead of time marching forward, it comes full circle.

Time, when viewed as a continuum, is a straight line with the past, present, and future occupying isolated and unrelated areas of separate space. When viewed as a circle or a spherical spiral, time revolves in a circular motion with the past, present, and future occupying the same space in interrelated vibrations of energy and matter. You can experience the simultaneous vibrations of time by stretching the circular motion of time through the spherical energies of space, matter, and motion.

Let's look into the future just a bit. By seeing into the future, you can alter your experiences before they seemingly occur because they are in the process of happening in the present in interrelated vibrations of energy. I have a plaque in my office with a beautiful picture of a rainbow. The plaque reads: "The past cannot be changed, but the future is whatever you want it to be." It's a nice sentiment, but I totally disagree with it. I believe that *the past can be changed to reflect whatever you want the future to be.* I believe it because I know it to be true, and many of my past-life regression clients and students in my reincarnation classes have found it to be true for themselves. Time is an illusion and becomes real only through your perceptions of it. A better, more accurate way to phrase the above sentiment would be: The past and the future can be changed to reflect whatever you want the present to be.

INTERACTIVE EXPERIENCE: FACING YOUR FUTURE

You can change the physical manifestations and expressions of experiences in future lives by going into your future experiences and changing them. You can put yourself into the future picture of your reality to change what hasn't happened yet in the future to correspond with experiences in your present and your past. It might help to see or become aware of things from a different perspective and frame of awareness from the way you usually view them and in the way they show themselves in the apparent logic or order of progression. Reverse the normal order of things.

Look at your picture of the past changed event from the previous chapter in reverse—from the future into the present, going into the past. See your life as a tapestry of motion that blends into the past, present, and future simultaneously. You'll be in the moving pictures of the future of your new, changed past experience to completely experience and understand all its interwoven energies. Then, pull the future energies into the present to create and change both your past and your future, whether it's yesterday, tomorrow, or eons away.

Watch the movie from the previous chapter in your mind's eye from a different perspective. Look a bit differently at the past experience that you changed as it shows itself on the movie screen, as you watch pieces of the future filter through the new, changed energies of the past as they show themselves in the present. You'll notice that your movie screen appears different. You see simultaneous, side-by-side time frames for viewing and experiencing events in your future lives alongside events in past lives to see how they interrelate, influence, and affect one another in the present. Put yourself in the center of the picture in both the past and the future.

You see how the future appears now because of the changed energies of your past experience, and you know that the changes you see in the future were actually there as vibrations of energy before you changed the past, even though it appeared that the energies of the event you changed in the past affected and changed the interrelated future energy vibrations of this past experience. Watch the future images of your new changed past experience as they appear on the screen.

Project yourself into the movie, into the future scenes, to see your thoughts, to hear your feelings, and to read the energy expressions of both the new changed past experience and the future repercussions of the changes you set into motion in your past experience. See how the future of this past experience, before you changed its energies, caused and created your present feelings about wanting to change the past. You'll see that the changes you made in the past were influenced by the future energy vibrations and expressions of the interrelated experiences that have already occurred in the future. You'll see that as you changed the past, you correspondingly changed the future. Or perhaps you'll see how the changed energies in the future orchestrated the changes in the past.

Now that you've viewed the energies of the past-future experience somewhat separately side by side, view the images of the past and future experience together as the images merge and blend into one another in the present. In the last chapter, you began to watch how the energies of the changed past experience—your new changed past experience—played out on the other side as you traveled into the future. But now you know that you're seeing a truer picture of how the future played out in the past and that while you were changing the past, you were also changing the future at the same time; you were changing events before they actually occurred.

This simultaneous movie screen in your mind—in addition to viewing past and future lives simultaneously in the present as your soul shows you the pictures—offers you wonderful opportunities for changing things in the present and thereby affecting, influencing, and changing things in the past that will—at the same time—cause the energy to reverberate and ripple through all the interrelated events to support, energize, and build the foundation for present and future experiences, and vice versa.

SEVEN

Looking Through the Spaces of Time to See Yourself

All your lives are lived at the same time in various vibrations of energy. You can shift your frame of awareness and focus of attention to meet your past and future selves, and to become aware of your probable selves by looking through the spaces of time to see yourself. You can interact with yourself in other lives and levels of awareness to share knowledge and become aware of events that influence your present life in unseen and unexpected ways. You can explore past lives to see the connection to your present and probable futures, while you're exploring future lives to view your probable present and past lives. You can change and create experiences in the past and the future and put those energies into motion in the present to become the probable self that you see.

In a linear manner, both the past and the present hold the shape and form of your personality in a probable future self. In one of my past lives, I was a writer. It's no surprise that in my present life I'm a writer. And it's a no-brainer that in a future life I'll probably be a writer. Because of being a writer in the past, I created the energy vibration to be a writer in the present so I could accomplish my soul's purpose, which was left unfinished the last time. At the same time in the past and the present, I also created and am creating the probability of being a writer in a future life.

Let's take linear time out of the picture. Let's suppose for a moment that reincarnation works in reverse—that future lives create present and past lives, instead of past lives creating your present life, and present life creating your future lives. Because I'm a writer in one of my future lives, that's why I'm also a writer in the present and the past. All these lives are happening simultaneously; that's why I'm phrasing them in the present tense. My future life as a writer created my present life as a writer so I could experience my past, which, in linear terms, carried over the energy vibrations for me being a writer in my present life.

From my present, I've had conversations with and revelations about the writer I was in one of my past lives. This particular past life is the one that most directly relates to and affects my present life because of the continuity of my soul's purpose this time, which is to teach and write about spiritual knowledge. The energies of that past life are in sync with the present energies of being a writer and a teacher. They're the interweaving threads that connect the past to the present.

Once I became aware, through a past-life regression, of the high priest-turned-philosopher that I was in Egypt and the traumatic experiences I'd had, I began to have conversations with him by looking through the spaces of time into the past. In that past life, he felt that the knowledge he cared so deeply about was lost. He/I had written a *Scroll of Knowledge* that contained the esoteric teachings he'd learned in Egypt as a high priest. By engaging in a mixture of in-depth meditations and shamanic journeying, I connected with him—with that past part of my soul—and felt his sadness and despair. It was like looking through a tunnel, then into a mirror. I told him that he was me now, that the knowledge hadn't been lost; I was rewriting it in the present from the knowledge he/I had acquired in Egypt. I showed him my second book, *Spirituality and Self-Empowerment*, which was a rewrite of the *Scroll of Knowledge.* By reconnecting with him, from his future, I was able to heal the pain and trauma of my past life in the present.

Your past lives are connected to your present life, just as your future lives are linked in the same way. It depends on what viewpoint you're looking at them from. When I connected with the philosopher, it was from his viewpoint of the future into my perception of the past. It was his future that established the link and enabled me to converse with him. It seemed that he was looking at me, rather than me looking at him, because he was looking into the future to resolve the trauma that triggered my actions of remembering and healing my past, even though at first I thought it was I becoming aware of him. In his/my past, he created his probable future/present as me.

People in my future-life workshops have seen previews of who they are/become and events that happen/are happening in their future lives relative to their present experiences (due to the interweaving threads of energy that connect the present and future together), in their dreams and through intuition—their inner knowing—as well as in future-life progressions.

One of my students, Sara, was studying to be a nurse; she was feeling quite discouraged, thinking she'd never make it. She was having a lot of problems with one of the classes and felt she wouldn't be a good nurse. Just as she was ready to quit school, she dreamed she was a doctor in a future life. In her dream, she talked with the doctor (her future self). He asked her to stay in school to become a nurse and create the healing pattern that would be continued in her future life as the doctor. He then helped her learn what she didn't understand in the class because he had already learned it in his future (his/her past/present).

This brings up an interesting idea. How could he know the answers in the future and be able to tutor her on what she was having problems with learning in the present? If she wasn't learning it in the present, how could he know it in the future? Wouldn't it seem logical that she would have to know it before he could know it also? Unless maybe he was studying or had studied it in the future, or in a parallel life, and it came easily to him, so he could then help her learn it.

A parallel life, either in the past or the future, or simultaneously in the present, closely resembles what you are experiencing in your present life, though events can get a little ahead or behind themselves. For example, the life of the philosopher I was in Egypt is parallel to the one I am experiencing now in the present. (More information on parallel lives is given in Chapter Eleven.)

You can look into other lives to see your actual past and future selves, based on who you are now, what you're doing, and what your soul needs and wants to experience. You can also become aware of your probable past and future selves by looking in the present at your thoughts, feelings, experiences, and actions because they contribute to creating who you probably will be in a future life. Probable past and future selves haven't been incarnated yet; you're shaping the energy of your past-future selves in the present. The energy is there for them to exist; it is wavering in the land of possibilities and probabilities. Whether or not they come into existence depends on what you do in the present and what you've done or are doing in the past. You create and bring your probable selves into being through your present thoughts, feelings, actions, and experiences.

As you're looking into a future life to see an actual future self, you may become aware that you're really looking at a probable self in one of your past lives. It often works in reverse because the nature of time doesn't fall into past, present, and future spaces. The difference between an actual past or future self, and a probable past or future self, is that your probable selves seem to come and go rather rapidly; they appear and disappear. Your actual past and future selves are much more solid; they have more substance, though they, too, are changeable through your actions, and by your thoughts and feelings in the present.

INTERACTIVE EXERCISES:
MEETING YOURSELF

You can meet your past and future selves and converse with them. You can see who you were and who you will become. This is similar to going back in time to talk with yourself as a child. You, as the child, perceive your present, adult self as a future self. It depends on which viewpoint or perspective you're looking from.

Visit a past and future self in the present by viewing yourself as a child from the adult point of view—from who you are now—then switch roles. As an adult, look into the past to see who you were. As a child, look into the future to see the adult you've become. As you're doing this, be aware of the interactions and feelings between the past and future parts of yourself.

Take this a bit further. Look into the future in this life to see the future self you'll become based on who you are now, what you're doing, your current experiences, and what you're thinking about doing. Then, from your future self in this lifetime, visit your present self—who you are now. This is the same way that you'll look into past and future selves in other lives.

When you're conversing with yourself, in the past or the future, you may become aware of changing places, as if your past or future self is talking to you, rather than you talking to your past or future self. Instead of you looking through your eyes to see them, they're looking through their eyes to see you. You may also switch roles; you may feel as if you are embodied in your past or future self instead of being your present self. It's an interesting feeling.

Another way you may experience past and future selves in this life or in past and future lives is by establishing a telepathic link with, or rapport between, your present self and your past and future selves. When you're tuned in to one of your past or future selves, it feels as if a current of energy is running between you and your other selves. Keep in mind that your past and future selves are part of your soul; this establishes the telepathic link and rapport between you.

You can meet some of your actual past and future selves; you can see and shape your probable selves. Actually, they're waiting to meet you and have been wondering why you haven't visited them yet. They will share insightful information and intuitive experiences with you to help you as you travel through the here and now of your present experiences, just as you can help them in their life by sharing information. After you meet and talk with them, you may discover that they're more aware of you right now than you are of them.

You can connect with them easily just by thinking about who you are right now and what is happening in your life. Think about the major events and experiences in your present life. Tune in to your feelings about them. These are the connecting links, the interweaving threads of energy between you and your past and future selves. Look through the spaces of time as you travel the energies of time into your past and future lives to meet and talk with yourself in other vibrations of time, to become aware of experiences that your soul has already had, is in the process of having, or will have. Take all the time you want and need in the following meditation to rediscover various parts of yourself in the past, the present, and the future.

SOUL-EXPANDING MEDITATION: RAINBOW ENERGIES

To meet your past and future selves, you'll travel through time on the energies of rainbow colors to trace the interweaving threads. Your soul vibrates to the energies of rainbow colors in several ways. Within your physical body are seven energy vortexes, called chakras, that vibrate to the colors of a rainbow—red, orange, yellow, green, blue, indigo (a deep purplish-blue), and violet. Your chakras are spinning disks or wheels of energy; they vibrate to various levels of awareness and experiences.

The first two—red and orange—vibrate to earthly, physical energy and emotions. The third—yellow—vibrates to intuition and inner knowing. Your heart chakra—green—is the center between earthly and spiritual energy, and vibrates to feelings. Blue, indigo, and violet vibrate to higher soul levels. Blue is the color of communication, indigo is the color of psychic awareness, and violet is the color of spirituality. As your chakras spin, they emit energy in the form of light.

Since everyone is individual and unique, and your experiences in past and future lives are widely diverse, it is difficult to generalize about what you may experience. That being said, you'll most likely find probable past and future selves in the vibrations of orange and yellow, while actual past and future selves vibrate mostly to blue and indigo. During this self-guided meditation, you'll be traveling the energies of your chakras to visit past and future selves within the strands of light. As you travel the waves and vibrations of light, you may astral project into past and future lives, feeling as if you were there rather than here in your present body.

Your past and future selves may appear in a bubble of light, or you may see them as physical beings who reach out to embrace you. You may find yourself in a beautiful place with many gardens; as you walk through the gardens, your past and future selves walk beside you and explain what you are experiencing in each garden. Each garden is a metaphor for a separate life. At the gate or entrance to the next garden, another part of your soul appears as a past or future self, and you continue your journey with that part of yourself. You may also be aware of a guide; this is your soul, perhaps embodied in a being of light or what you may perceive as an angel.

One of my clients, Sam, experienced what he called a "blue light special." As he was going through the rainbow to meet his past and future selves, he saw a spiritual guide—what he thought was an angel, who was a being of light radiating thousands of blue sparkles of light that were constantly moving and changing shape. She took him by the hand and led him into the interim between lives, where he saw the reasons for and purpose of his present life, and how he was connected to other souls in this lifetime that he had made soul promises to. The being of blue light then showed him the future self that his soul wanted him to be in this lifetime in order to shape and become the future self he already was in a future life.

As you rise upward through the rainbow, absorbing and immersing yourself in each color, you will feel drawn to certain colors; you will feel an affinity with that color. When you feel this, breathe in and be the color. Surround yourself completely with the color. When you are vibrating to the energies of the color, you will see or sense strands of vibrating light that are emitted from within you. Travel these strands of light to meet your past and future selves. You may also find that the color you are in changes to another color within your experiences. If you want to enter spiritual energies to see the higher aspects of your soul in past and future lives, travel through the energies of violet.

We tend to continue and carry over the things we enjoy just as much as we continue and carry over bad karma until it's balanced. Some of your past and future selves might not be nice people. If at any time you feel uncomfortable with a past or future self, immediately go above the rainbow into the white mist of the universe. The white mist is a universal light that is warm, safe, peaceful, and protecting. Breathe in and be the white light; it is the spiritual light of your soul. Then talk with these past and future selves. These not-so-nice parts of your soul may help you in a beneficial way.

Begin your meditation by just breathing normally. As you breathe in, inhale peaceful, quiet feelings of relaxation. As you breathe out, let go of tension and tightness from your body. Focus on your breathing; let your breath bring you into the inner knowing of your soul's awareness. When you feel comfortably relaxed, calm, and peaceful within yourself, imagine a very beautiful rainbow above you that is shimmering and sparkling with energy.

Travel the energies of each color within the rainbow to become aware of your past and future selves. Spend some time within each color to see the past and future selves that appear, or the probable selves you become aware of. When you are with them, talk with them; ask them questions. Interact with them. Don't be shy; you're meeting and talking with yourself in another vibration of time, in another space of energy. Explore everything you see and become aware of. Your past and future selves are part of you, part of your soul; it's easy to get in touch with them and communicate with all these parts of yourself.

SIGNIFICANT PAST-FUTURE SOULS

Souls tend to reincarnate together. If you've had a love relationship with a particular soul in the past, more than likely you'll be with that person again; you may be in a different relationship, or the souls you know now may be in the same roles. Your husband now may be your wife in a future lifetime. Your mother may have been your sister in the past and your best friend in the future. Your son or daughter may be your brother or your father. We switch roles in other lifetimes to have well-rounded experiences and to see all sides.

You can explore past and future relationships with your loved ones. Look into probable futures with your present friends and lovers to see where your souls will be, together or separate, in the future. Think about a special someone who is in your life right now. More than likely you've known him or her in past lives and your bond is strong. It's also very likely that you'll be with this person again in future lifetimes. There's a love connection between you; your spirits are joined in a timeless realm of emotion.

The energies of love are very powerful; they continue strongly through time. You can meet and talk with a special someone you're with now in the past and the future, just as you met and spoke with your past and future selves. To see how and where this soul fits into a future life with you, travel the rainbow again. Follow the flow of your heart chakra.

As you're traveling on the light energies of the color green that radiate within and emanate from your heart chakra, you'll also see how the souls you're connected with now as friends and family appear in your past and future lives. You may or may not be with your current family and friends, or your special someone, in a future life no matter how much you want to be. This is because someone else's free will is involved. Being with a certain person again is only a probability, not a definite thing. It depends on what both of your souls need and have agreed to experience, together or separately, to evolve.

Think about your special someone and tune in to the energy vibration that connects your souls together. Feel the love you have between you. Feel it vibrating inside your heart. Center in on the color green—your heart chakra—the energy of love. Travel the strands of light and love to see how your special someone appears in your future life. When you're with him or her, spend some time with this special soul who is so very important to you and interact with him or her. As you do this, you will also be affecting the present energies of your relationship, as well as your future-life relationship. Bring these future feelings of love and harmony into your present life to enhance your current relationship.

What holds true for friends and lovers appearing in your future lives also holds true for souls you're experiencing problems with now and ones you have karmic conflicts with. Your enemies will pop into your future lives just as often as, if not more than, your friends and lovers will. It depends on a great number of factors, two of the more important being your interactions with them in the present as well as the past, and the unspoken agreements made among you in the interim between lives when you were both choosing what you want and need to experience to grow your souls and resolve your karma.

You can see how and where your enemies show up in your probable future and past lives in which they will appear in order to resolve the karmic conflicts you have between you and bring about a beautiful balancing. I know it's not much fun, but think about the people you have problems with; explore the energy connection between you, and see how both your future and past experiences play out with them.

Travel the energies of red and orange to find your enemies. Once you pull them into your energy frame of awareness, you can resolve a great number of difficulties with them in your mind rather than having actual physical experiences with them in the energies of probable past and future experiences or your ongoing present.

If you want to balance the shared karma now, without carrying it over and having it play out in the past and/or the future, take your enemy by the hand into the white light above the rainbow. Talk with him or her to discover your soul agreements and then balance your karma in a loving, positive manner. When you resolve negative karmic situations in your mind and put your whole heart and soul into it, you're affecting the energies of those experiences in a much greater and more far-reaching way than you may be aware of now. When your karma is resolved in the spiritual energies of white light, take your enemy-who-is-now-a-friend into the color green in the rainbow to completely heal the relationship with him or her.

Your mind—your soul—is the energy link to all your past, present, and future selves and their experiences. Within every energy vibration of the rainbow, you'll become aware of a great many things about yourself and your experiences. You can do anything you want within the timeless energy of your mind in harmony with your soul.

EIGHT

Reexperiencing the Future in the Present-Past

If you could pull the future into the present, what would you do with what you learned, and how would it affect you? You may already know the answer to this from meeting your future selves in the previous chapter. What would you bring back from the future as a gift to yourself in the present? By bringing the future into the present, what corresponding changes would ripple through the past, present, and future? You can look into a future life to see how your present experiences and your past ones would change to support and frame your future experiences. You can look into a future life to see pictures of your future experiences, to observe your soul patterns, and to see the talents and abilities you have, and then weave them into both the past and present.

We've already worked with the thought *if I knew then what I know now* to bring the future into the present. Let's take that thought in a slightly different direction. You can go into a future life now to see whatever it is you see and bring that information back from the future to help you now. You can change, create, un-create, shape, form, or mold what hasn't happened yet in the present to correspond with what is happening or has already happened in the future. As you're in the process of observing pictures of events and patterns of your soul in the future, you can change and create whatever you want so that it is reflected in your present life.

If you like what you see in the future, you can bring those energies into the present to help you in any way you desire. This is the gift that you give yourself; it's similar to dream-weaving. When you want to learn or do something in the present, you weave it into your night dreams or a meditation in which you experience and accomplish it and then bring it forth in your life. This is what Sara did in Chapter Seven when she dreamed about herself as the future doctor.

Dream-weaving is the same thing as looking into a future life to bring something back with you into your present life that you've already accomplished in a future life. Julie attended a future-life workshop to see what she'd be doing in her future life and what she'd be like. Before I tell you what Julie saw and experienced in her future life, let me build the background. She was a student in my psychic awareness class who wanted to develop her intuitive powers; she was particularly interested in developing her healing ability. During the discussion before the future-life progression, I never mentioned auras (which are energy fields that surround a person; the colors vibrate in tune with the person's state of health and level of well-being) or suggested that the color meditation we'd be doing for the progression would help my students learn how to see and read auras. Actually, it never occurred to me to mention it, as we were going to be exploring future lives. Learning how to see and read auras wasn't scheduled for another few weeks in the psychic awareness class.

During the progression part of the workshop, Julie experienced a future life in which she saw herself as what she called a "divinator." A divinator is the equivalent of a psychic reader/faith healer in today's terminology. Before the workshop, she didn't have any desire to be a psychic reader or a faith healer; she just wanted to know what her future life was going to be.

After she experienced—or reexperienced, as the case may be—her future life, she wove the knowledge and ability she had acquired as a divinator in her future life into her present life. A week or so after the workshop, she said she could see and read auras to determine the health of a person, and she intuitively knew how to balance a person's aura by flowing white light into it to cleanse the aura and to create health and harmony in a person's physical energy vibrations. It's important to note that she'd had no desire to read auras before she explored her future life but did have a desire to help heal people, though she didn't see herself becoming a faith healer in this lifetime.

Abilities that you've developed in future lives can be brought into both your present and past lives in the same way that talents and skills from your past lives are carried over into your present life. For example, let's say you were a musician in a past life. In your present life, you're a whiz at composing symphonies. Presumably, you acquired this ability in a past life and carried it forward, which is why you're so good at it now.

Let's change that scenario a bit. Let's say that in this lifetime you're struggling to be a musician, writing notes and composing lyrics to songs. What if your struggles now to compose music pay off in the future? Wouldn't it be great to go into a future life to see the accomplished results of what you're learning in this lifetime, carrying over and further developing in a future life, and then bring that future knowledge, ability, and skill into your present life so you could compose better songs and write better music?

Think about something, a talent or an ability, that you'd like to develop further in this life, or a career you'd like to pursue. You have a strong desire to achieve what you want but wish you had the training so that your talent or ability was fully developed now. You can go into your future life to see the payoff of the efforts you've put forth, or will put forth, in this life. You can bring your talents and abilities that you've learned in the future into the present and reap the rewards now.

MIND-OPENING MEDITATION: MULTICOLORED PICTURES AND PATTERNS

This multicolored meditation focuses on future-life experiences and soul patterns. For example, if you're an artist or are trying to be an artist, perhaps you'll see images of pictures you'll paint in a future life or in the future in this life. If you want to learn how to do something, or even if you have no idea that you want to learn it, perhaps you'll see experiences framed in the present that reflect what you're going to be doing in a future life or later in the future in this lifetime, or you'll see just the opposite. Maybe you'll see future scenes that show you what to do in the present to meet and match your future.

The meditation will also show you soul patterns, such as a difficulty in a relationship or a personality trait, that have been carried over from the past into the present and will be continued and carried over into the future if the pattern or karma is not changed. As the colors change and blend into one another, you'll be aware of the vibrations of your soul patterns; they will draw a picture for you.

The following multicolor meditation will completely relax you, guiding you into a meditative frame of mind to open up your inner spiritual knowing as it leads you into the energies of your future-life experiences through the vibrations of the colors and the patterns they form in your mind. It's a gentle merging of rainbow colors in which you will experience the unique hues and vibrations of the colors as they blend and change into one another. There's no clear-cut distinction between the colors; they flow gradually into one another. Incorporated within the energies of the colors are the events and emotions in your future lives.

Go slowly through this meditation and pause whenever you want, so that you can completely experience what you become aware of. Allow the colors and their vibrations to form images in your mind. It might be a good idea to either record this meditation so you can listen to it, or have a friend read it to you so you can more completely experience the colors and the patterns of your soul as they portray themselves in your mind.

By experiencing and exploring all the hues and nuances—the tones and shades of each color—and by seeing how each vibrates, fluctuates, and moves in your perception, you'll see how each picture and pattern of your soul is interwoven in future experiences as they are in the process of being and becoming or as they have already been. You'll see how the changing pictures and patterns create and show you the experiences of your soul even as you change the patterns and pictures that you see.

As your awareness is flowing into and through the colors, tune in to them. Let yourself be the colors, experiencing and understanding the unique properties, qualities, and energy vibrations of each color—experiencing and understanding your future experiences within each color. Feel how each color blends and softly merges into another to see how your inner awareness and the essence of your soul—and all that it has experienced, is experiencing, or will experience in the future—blends your present thoughts, feelings, and experiences. You'll be tuning in to your spiritual knowing within the multidimensional energies of the colors to see the patterns of your soul and pictures of events in your future lives. Go with the flow of what you see, feel, and experience. Let your soul speak to you and show you the pictures and patterns of the future.

Begin this meditation by simply getting comfortable and closing your eyes. Breathe for a few moments as you begin to relax. The meditation will relax you into a higher level of awareness as the colors focus your mind inward toward your spiritual knowing. Take a deep breath in, feeling it fill you, then let it out slowly, feeling your body begin to relax, feeling your mind begin to open up and become more aware. Allow yourself to become attuned to what you're going to experience as you travel into the future through the nuances and hues, shades and tones of rainbow colors, as you travel into the awareness and knowing of your soul. Just continue to breathe naturally.

Center in and focus your awareness on the color red. Imagine the color red, feel the color red, and see the color red as you look toward the inner part of your mind. You'll begin to notice small fragments of color. At first, the color may seem to come and go, but as you relax more with every breath you take, the color comes more clearly into focus. The color pulsates in a relaxing rhythm, a subtle tone and hue of its color. You see that the color red begins to form a pattern and shows you pictures of future experiences as it vibrates in tune with your breathing.

As you focus on the color red, the color begins to change as your mind begins to expand into a more aware level. The color changes in intensity and hue, going toward a lighter color of red, a rosy-pink color that paints pictures of future life experiences and shows you your soul patterns in your mind. You're aware of your breathing and your feeling of relaxation; you're aware of your body vibrations and how they are beginning to change. You're aware of focusing your mind inward, seeing the soul patterns and your future experiences that the colors bring forth.

As you become more relaxed and more aware, the soul patterns and future pictures of the color red begin to blend into a light red and now into pink. You're aware that your breathing has become deep and regular, slow and rhythmic, matching your body vibrations. You feel the gentle vibrations of the colors wash over you and through you at the same time as you watch the pictures and patterns of light red and pink in your mind. You notice that the color pink begins to interact with the color orange as it forms moving patterns and pictures in your mind. You feel your body becoming more relaxed and your mind becoming more aware.

The color orange comes more clearly into focus and begins to form unusual and distinct pictures and patterns of color on the inner part of your mind, in the inner part of your spiritual awareness—your soul's inner knowing. The color pulsates in a rhythm that matches your body vibrations and your breathing.

With every breath you take, you notice that the color and the soul patterns and future-life pictures that it draws change with the rhythm of your breathing, change with the rhythm of your soul and your inner awareness. As you continue to relax and open up your inner knowing, the color begins to form more unusual patterns and pictures in your mind.

As you focus clearly on the color orange and the pictures and patterns that it draws, you direct your awareness more inward and become more in tune with yourself, more in tune with your spiritual vibrations. As the color draws you within and you continue to breathe evenly and deeply, the color begins to blend into a light orange, and now into a peach color, each color forming its own pictures and patterns, blending and vibrating in a rhythm that matches your body vibrations and your breathing.

With each breath you take, the colors change with your breathing. As you breathe in, you're more aware of the light orange color. As you breathe out, you're more aware of the peach color. The pictures and patterns of the colors continue to shift back and forth in a gentle, rhythmic motion, flowing from light orange to peach. You feel a sense of lightness in your body, and you're aware of your body's vibrations and your mind's awareness in relation to the colors and the pictures and patterns they form. All the day's tensions and anxieties, worries and cares flow from your body as if they were being drawn off into the air; they just float away as you focus your mind more inward, as you tune in to the vibrations of your soul.

You see that the light orange and peach colors have now blended into the color yellow, the color of sunshine, the color of knowledge. The soul patterns and future pictures of the color yellow focus clearly in your mind. As you go more within your mind, you become more aware. You feel so relaxed, much more relaxed than you felt before, as the color yellow forms intricate and unusual patterns and pictures in your mind, moving in a natural, easy rhythm that matches your body vibrations and your breathing, showing you pictures and patterns of experiences and events in your future lives that you can bring back with you into your present life.

You see both the inner and outer vibrations of the color. As you become more aware of the color yellow, you become more aware of your inner knowing, more in tune with your soul's awareness. With each breath you take, the soul patterns and future pictures become more clear and distinct, more detailed and descriptive. The patterns and pictures of the color yellow focus clearly in your mind. As you flow into a more aware level of mind, you focus your awareness more and more inward.

The gentle mixture of the orange, peach, and yellow colors now blends into a very beautiful, warm, golden color as you enter an even more aware level of mind, as you watch the future pictures and soul patterns that the golden color draws inside your mind and soul.

You feel so relaxed, more relaxed than you felt before. You feel very calm, tranquil, and at peace with yourself. You're aware of your breathing and your body vibrations; you're aware of tuning in to your inner knowing and your soul's awareness. You go even more inward, into a more aware level of mind, feeling more relaxed, more in tune with your breathing and your body vibrations. As you continue to flow into your inner awareness, your body feels very, very relaxed, so very pleasantly and deeply relaxed.

As you focus your inner awareness on the golden color, you notice that the patterns and pictures of the color begin to change; they begin to form more unusual and detailed patterns and pictures in your mind. With each breath you take, the patterns and pictures of your future experiences change in rhythm and harmony with your vibrations, in rhythm and harmony with your soul's awareness.

The golden color becomes part of you, just as you become part of the color, as the patterns and pictures in your future life become part of your inner knowing and your soul's awareness. You're in a much more aware level of mind now, where you're open and receptive to your inner knowing and your soul's awareness of your future experiences, and to how you can bring the pictures and patterns into your present life, weaving them into your current experiences, thoughts, and feelings.

You feel the golden color vibrating all around you and within you. The color forms a more rhythmic pattern, more clear and detailed, more focused, matching the pattern of your inner spiritual awareness as you enter even more aware levels of mind to see the pictures and patterns of your soul's future experiences. Within the golden color, you see the soul patterns and the pictures of events that you will experience in your future life; you see the patterns and pictures of events that have already happened in the future and ones that are in the process of happening right now in the future.

Your inner mind, your soul, knows that time in a spiritual vibration is measured in a flowing, fluid movement of energy that moves in a circular, rhythmic pattern. As you continue through the vibrations of the colors, through the future pictures and soul patterns that they draw, your inner knowing and spiritual awareness continues to become more clear and focused, showing you the patterns of your soul within your experiences, showing you the pictures of events and emotions, talents and abilities, in your future life—patterns, events and emotions, talents and abilities—that you can bring with you into the present as you weave them into your awareness.

Notice how the golden color has slowly and softly changed to the color green. Even as you watch the pictures and patterns that it draws, and become in tune with the color's subtle hues and nuances, with the hues and nuances of your future experiences, the color changes to the most beautiful, vivid green that you've ever imagined could exist.

The pure green color that you're seeing is somewhat of a new experience for you because it vibrates to spiritual energies, rather than to physical energies. But it's not really a new shade of green. You've seen this color before in your soul's awareness, in your soul's travels through time and space. Your inner mind and your soul remember the pure spiritual vibrations of this color and how the soul patterns and future pictures inside this color interact with and weave through your spiritual awareness of your physical experiences.

As you continue through the colors, you experience an expanded awareness in each color, in the patterns and vibrations, in the shades and tones, hues and nuances of each color, in the pictures of each experience your soul will have in the future. The patterns come clearly into focus for you as you picture the color green inside your mind, as you feel the color vibrating inside your soul. You see individual pictures and patterns of the color green, the color of health, the color of healing, the color of growth, the color of harmony, the color that rises above your physical energies even as it interacts with your physical awareness, showing you the spiritual energy vibrations of your physical experiences, both now and as they are interwoven in a future life.

You feel your mind and your body vibrating to the energies of the color green. The healing color of green enters inside you and flows into and through your physical body; it enters and flows into your mind as you become more in tune with yourself, more aware of the spiritual awareness and knowing that you have within. The patterns and pictures that form in your mind are very clear and focused. In essence, you have become the color green, with all of its healing abilities for your body, mind, and soul.

With every breath you take, the pure color of green surrounds you and enters you, revitalizing and rejuvenating your physical body as you become completely relaxed, as you become completely in tune with the vibrations of green, completely in tune with your soul's awareness. The pure, spiritual color of green that you're now seeing and feeling surrounds you and encircles you as it simultaneously flows into and through you, like a rhythmic heartbeat. Bring the color more inward, more inside you, as you continue to enter a more aware, more spiritual level of mind.

The color blends into your body and your mind, into your heart and soul, producing more vivid pictures and patterns than before. The color green gently moves in a soft, easy, natural rhythm with your breathing, flowing into and through your mind's awareness, into and through your body vibrations, healing you from the inside out, harmonizing your vibrations as you enter into the spiritual knowing and awareness of your soul. Your body feels much lighter than it did before, much healthier and more relaxed. You may even feel as if your body is no longer part of you because you're so much more in tune with your spiritual vibrations.

Breathing and being in tune with your spiritual vibrations, feeling relaxed and aware, you see that the pure color of green is now beginning to change, its nuances and hues, shades and tones of its future pictures and soul patterns beginning to flow into the color blue, changing the color green as it flows into various shades of blue. You notice the color blue more clearly, as fragments and highlights of the color blue begin to blend with the color green to draw pictures and patterns of future experiences in your mind.

The color blue begins to change the color green, turning it into the most beautiful color of blue-green you've ever seen and experienced in both your physical experiences and your spiritual awareness. The two colors swirl together in a soft, gentle rhythmic pattern and vibration, forming intricate and detailed pictures. The colors move together in a circular rhythm and pattern, larger and smaller, lighter and darker.

The blue and green colors change with the rhythm of your breathing. As you breathe in, the colors become a deep blue-green. As you breathe out, they become lighter blue and green, turning to a light aquamarine turquoise, then returning to shades and nuances of blue and green. As the soul patterns and future pictures of the colors continue to shift back and forth, you feel as if you're by the ocean watching the tide ebb and flow, watching the water as it comes to the shore, light blue-green in color; and watching the water as it returns to the ocean, dark blue-green in color. You're breathing in tune with the soft, easy rhythm of the waves, with the rhythm of time, with the rhythm and harmony of your soul.

It seems as if the two colors are really one color. They blend together to form a color that is a mixture of aqua-blue and sea-green. The colors ebb and flow as your breathing and inner awareness move rhythmically in tune with your soul's awareness. You see a blending rhythmic pattern that flows in harmony with your future experiences. The pictures from the future focus more clearly in your mind, and the colors are much more clear.

Standing on the seashore, looking out toward the ocean and upward toward the sky, you see clearly all around you, as you look toward the horizon in all directions, knowing that you can see well beyond the horizon into your future experiences, knowing that your soul's awareness is showing you the pictures and patterns of experiences in your future life through the colors of your soul and the energy vibrations of the colors.

The color blue begins to emerge from the mixture of blue-green. At first, it seems that the colors are almost the same, with only a slight distinction in hue between them, but you notice more of the blue color as you enter a more open, aware, spiritual level of knowing within your mind. You see well beyond the horizon into future pictures and soul patterns. You feel as if you could reach up and touch the sky; you're so very aware of the blue sky that surrounds you like a beautiful dome. You can see from end to end and you're aware that the sky is not a dome, that it doesn't end where your physical perception of it ends. It extends far beyond what your physical eyes can see, the sky opening up and inviting you to travel into higher spiritual vibrations of your inner knowing and soul awareness.

The color blue, the color of the sky, brings forth within you a feeling of total serenity, a perfect feeling of total peace, harmony, and tranquility. You know that you're traveling on the energy of your soul up into and through the sky. Focusing more on the sky above you, you become more aware of the color blue, with all its subtle tones and shades, its nuances and hues. You feel yourself becoming part of the color as the color becomes part of you. You see the pictures and patterns of the color blue as you watch the pictures and patterns of your future experiences.

You're breathing in and breathing out the color blue. The color has become part of you; you are the color blue, the color of the sky, the color of peace and serenity, the color of communication between your soul's awareness and your physical consciousness. The color blue opens a channel of communication between your soul and your mind, between the future and the present.

As you continue to look upward and to travel above the sky, the color blue softly and slowly changes in its hue and vibration, in the changing soul patterns and future pictures you see within the color. You feel your inner vibrations change as you feel your inner knowing and spiritual awareness opening up even more. As you enter a higher level of spiritual awareness, you see that the sky begins to change color as you begin to go through the sky and rise above it.

The sky begins to change first to a deeper color blue, then the color begins to change even more, turning into the color indigo, a deep purplish blue, as you become more aware of your inner knowledge and your spiritual awareness, as you become more aware of the soul patterns and pictures of future experiences that you can bring with you into the present.

You feel as if you're flying above the Earth, into and through the universe. You notice that you are forming the pictures and patterns from your soul's inner knowing as you journey through and above the sky that is turning into the color indigo. You're forming the pictures and patterns of the colors now. You're seeing the pictures and patterns of experiences that your soul has already created and drawn; you're seeing the pictures and patterns as they change vibration and weave into your awareness. You're directing the patterns and pictures that the colors inspire and bring forth within you. You're directing the pictures and patterns from a higher level of your soul's awareness. As you see what your spiritual awareness is showing you, you become even more aware of the spiritual knowing that you have within you, even more aware of the pictures and patterns that your soul has drawn and is drawing for you to see and experience.

As you watch the soul patterns and future pictures of the color indigo, and as you become part of the color, part of the future pictures and soul patterns you see as you immerse yourself in your future experiences, the color begins to change to purple. As your energy vibrations begin to change in the subtle tones, nuances, shades, and hues of the color purple, you enter an even more aware level of mind beyond the sky, beyond the boundaries of space and time.

You become more in tune with the color purple, seeing the future pictures and soul patterns of purple. You become more in rhythm and harmony with the energies within you, and more aware of, and in tune with, the vibrations of your true spiritual nature. You know that you're expanding your spiritual awareness and inner knowing above the sky into the universe, expanding your soul's inner knowing into and above the horizons that open up and expand more and more. You feel as if you could reach out and embrace the universe and breathe it inside you.

The vibrations and hues of the color purple softly surround you and enter you, flowing into your mind's awareness, flowing into your soul, rising into an even higher level of mind. The soul patterns and future pictures move gently through your feelings and inside your mind, in harmony with your inner knowing and with your spiritual awareness, rhythmically changing the patterns and pictures that move in tune with your vibrations, with the vibrations of your future experiences.

You notice that the soul patterns and future pictures you form with the color purple are all of a spiritual nature and that they put you more in touch with your true inner nature, in tune with your spiritual awareness. You become aware of a natural rhythm and harmony that moves within your mind, within your inner knowing, as you go even more inward into your spiritual essence, into the patterns and pictures of your soul.

The nuances of the color purple become clearer and more focused within your feelings and your mind as you see and experience more of your spiritual nature, as you draw the purple color within you. The patterns and pictures flow and change as you go even more inward into your soul. You have a complete understanding of your spiritual nature as the color purple begins to change to violet, turning lighter and lighter in color from purple to violet. You're in rhythm and harmony with your spiritual nature; you're much more aware of your spiritual inner knowing and all the knowledge you have within yourself of the experiences and events in your future lives.

The soul patterns and future pictures of violet blend into a smooth, gentle, natural rhythm that matches the vibrations of your spiritual awareness. You're aware of the nuances and hues in the color, in the shades and hues, in the vibrations of the patterns and pictures that the color portrays.

You become aware of a white light that softly enters from all directions to change the color of violet. This light seems to emanate from the universe and from within you at the same time; it changes the patterns and pictures that you see and sense, that you know and feel. The white light begins to change the color violet into a lighter color of violet, as you go more within your mind, more within your spiritual essence, as you see the future pictures and patterns of your soul, as you become more completely in tune with your spiritual nature.

As you absorb the changing, blending colors of the various shades and hues of violet into your mind and soul, you feel a flowing, rhythmic sensation in harmony with the vibrations of the color's nuances. You're breathing them in and out as your vibrations move in perfect rhythm and harmony with the colors, as they form the future patterns and pictures that you see and understand with your mind and your soul.

The white light that emanates from both the universe and within you, within your soul, is becoming brighter and clearer. The vibrations move within your mind as they blend into your feelings, as they blend with the colors and patterns and pictures you form and perceive with your inner awareness, with your spiritual knowing. The various colors of violet are clear and distinct, yet they continuously and softly change in their intensity and vibration, in their nuance and hue, as you continue to see and travel through the pictures and patterns of your soul's awareness.

The future pictures and soul patterns, and the vibrations of the violet colors, continue to slowly shift back and forth, gently moving in rhythm and harmony with your spiritual knowing. At first, the various shades of violet waver and fluctuate at the same time, then they change to a lighter color of violet, moving gently within and through you as you focus more clearly on the color with your soul. The various hues of violet fluctuate and move together, blending naturally, then turning lighter in color as the white light blends into violet, as you focus your awareness even more inward, as you become more in tune with the vibrations of your spiritual essence.

The violet color flows softly on your breath, in harmony with the white light, turning into a lavender color that then blends into a very beautiful mixture of violet and lavender. The future pictures and soul patterns that you see are very delicate; they seem to disappear and reappear with every breath you take, becoming clearer as you focus your mind's awareness on the colors of violet and lavender, as you focus your soul's knowing more inward and above yourself into the light, as you become more in tune with the rhythm of your soul.

The patterns and pictures of the violet and lavender colors blend into your mind, into your feelings, into your soul. As you absorb the colors within, as you perceive the future pictures and soul patterns within, you enter a very aware level of mind—a spiritual frame of awareness—where you're in perfect harmony with the vibrations of your soul.

You feel a total peace of mind, a total serenity within yourself, within your soul. You feel completely in tune with your spiritual nature, knowing that your soul has the rhythms and patterns within itself of the pictures of all your experiences, and that this is what you are seeing. You are looking through your soul at the pictures and patterns in your future life. As this feeling, this knowing, becomes stronger and stronger, you become more aware of and in tune with the white light that begins to change the color of lavender, turning it lighter and lighter as you go more inward in your mind, more inward in your soul.

As you focus your awareness on the light that radiates and emanates both from within you and all around you, you become more aware of the pictures and patterns of the lavender color as it flows into the color of white—a very pure white light that forms the most intricate and unusual patterns and pictures as you enter the most aware level of your soul's inner knowing. You feel the white color being absorbed into your body, mind, and soul. As this color of pure white is absorbed within you and becomes part of you, part of the feelings inside you, part of your soul's aware-ness, part of your inner knowing, you see that the future pictures and the patterns of your soul become completely clear, totally focused, and much more intricate in design and variation.

You feel yourself vibrating to the color of white, the color of purity, the color of your soul. All the knowledge of the universe is within you; it is part of you, and you are part of all the knowl-edge of the universe. You feel a positive attunement with all that is around you and within you as you experience the unity of your mind and soul, the unity of the Earth with the universe, the unity of your spiritual nature with the pictures and patterns of your future life. You're in the most aware level of mind, where all your spiritual knowledge is available to you. You're perfectly in tune with the rhythm of your spiritual vibrations, and you know that your soul is in complete harmony with the white light of the universe.

Absorbing the white color within your mind, within your soul, you see the unique patterns, the unique pictures that the color forms in your mind of your future experiences that have been, now are, and have yet to be. Within the white color, you feel your *soul vibrating in harmony with itself. You're in your spiritual essence; you're inside your soul. You have a complete understanding of all the pictures and patterns you've seen and experienced in the future. And you know that incorporated within the white light—within each variation, shade, tone, and hue of every color—are the rhythms and patterns of future experiences; future experiences that you can bring the energies of into your present life, weaving them into your present experiences.*

As you breathe in the white light and draw it inside you, you become fully aware of and completely understand all the pictures and patterns in your future life; you are fully aware of everything you saw, felt, experienced, and became aware of in each color. Explore and experience all that you see and know in every vibration of every color, in every vibration of every experience. Bring these future pictures and soul patterns that your soul is showing you within yourself—into your mind, into your physical consciousness. Bring the awareness and knowledge of everything you have experienced in all the future pictures and soul patterns of every vibration of color into your present life to help you in any way your soul desires.

As you traveled through the rainbow energies into the future, you traveled into and through the energies of your soul. This is a natural, inborn ability that you have. You can journey within your soul at any time you want to and for any reason. The pictures and patterns that your soul has shown you in this meditation are gifts from the future; gifts that you can use in your present life.

NINE

Fragments of the Future

Y ou already know how to see fragments of your future lives. In this chapter, let's stay in the present to see the fragments of your future in *this* life. Seeing the future in this life shows you how to look into your future lives. The only difference is that your future lives may appear to be a little bit more out of your reach than the future in the present. But that's not really true; that's only the way it seems.

Images of experiences in the future often show themselves in flashes of precognition, in feelings of intuition, and in your dreams. You also become aware of events in the future through a daydream, a reverie, or a focused meditation. When you tune in to your intuition, engage in a meditation, or dream, you're tuned in to your subconscious mind and you have access to all the spiritual knowing inside you. Your dreams transcend time and space; they show you pictures of the past, present, and future simultaneously. The past, the present, and the future are all happening at the same time as you experience them in your dream.

Perhaps you've had an experience of knowing that something was going to occur, and what it was, before it happened. You may have picked up feelings or vibes about it or seen information about the future event within a dream or in your mind's eye. This is called precognition, which is defined as "previous knowing or awareness; perception of an event, condition, etc., before it occurs."

You've looked into the future to see what was going to happen. When you're aware of something before it happens, you're outside the realm of linear time. If this future something hasn't happened yet, how do you know it's going to occur? Did you mind-trip through time into the future? Was your awareness in the future at the same time it was in the present? Or is it because the future exists now and you tuned in to that vibration of energy? How could you be aware of something that hasn't happened yet, unless it is happening in the future at the same time that you become aware of it in the present? Precognition is an inherent spiritual ability that shows you that your future experiences exist now in another wavelength of energy, vibrating in harmony with the present and the past, perhaps paralleling one another.

People have looked into the future in this lifetime and seen events that were going to happen. Consider the novel *Futility* by Morgan Robertson. Fictional events and descriptions in the novel closely paralleled what actually occurred fourteen years later when the *Titanic* sailed into that fatal iceberg. There have been many prophets and psychics who have predicted future events with astonishing accuracy. Looking into the future is an ability we all have within us. It's not such a stretch to look a bit further than the present future into a future lifetime. They both work the same way.

You also become aware of events in future lives intuitively. Precognition is closely linked to intuition, which is your sense of inner knowing. Intuition is an innate ability; it's a characteristic of your subconscious, more spiritually aware mind. It is defined as "the direct knowing of something without the conscious use of reasoning; immediate understanding; the ability to perceive or know things without conscious reasoning." Your conscious mind functions on things in the physical, three-dimensional world. Your subconscious mind is on a different wavelength; it functions on things in the realm of spiritual reality. It houses your soul memories of both the past and the future.

Your dreams also show you that your future coexists with your present. I met a friend in my dreams and traveled with him twice on an astral level before I actually met him in person. I'd been doing some serious shamanic work on soul retrieval. During my dream, I was flying, going into a past life in which I had left part of my soul, and this guy appeared and was flying next to me. He asked if I wanted to go into an entrance to a tree. I told him to leave me alone because I already had somewhere to go. I did some astral maneuvers to get away from him. I eluded him and continued on my astral journey.

The next night he appeared again. He said he could help me with my soul retrieval. Then he flew away. A few weeks later, I attended a drumming ceremony, which is designed to guide you into non-ordinary levels of reality. When the shaman explained the journey we'd be going on, he said that we would enter the lower world through an entrance to a tree. When he said that, I remembered that I'd met him before; he'd been in my dreams. During the drumming journey, I went deeper into my past life and over the next few days completed my soul retrieval. He'd helped me, just as he'd said he could in the dream. Because I had dreamed about him and the events connected with him before they occurred, I was in my future before I was in my present.

As physical beings, we function in a three-dimensional reality of past, present, and future. This is how we perceive time happening in our physical reality; anything that differs from that, we perceive to be an illusion, something that isn't real because it isn't a concrete, logical thing and we can't wrap our conscious mind around it. When we become aware of an event in the future within a dream, a reverie, in our thoughts, or in a meditation, time doesn't exist in the context of our physical, three-dimensional concept of time. Dreams, precognition, reveries, meditations, intuition, and inner knowing—your spiritual awareness—work on wavelengths of energy that wend and weave their way through your subconscious mind into your conscious awareness.

Energy is always active, always in motion. Often we aren't aware of all the vibrations of the future, so the energy seems empty, as if it doesn't exist yet. We believe that the future exists and that it will occur, because past experience has proven that it always does. We just don't consciously think it's happening right now. When we look, with limited physical awareness, into the future, there appears to be nothing there, yet sometimes we sense a feeling of potential energy that is swirling around, formless and without direction, floating through empty spaces.

On the other hand, sometimes we're very aware of experiences in the future in this lifetime, and in our future lives, without consciously knowing that we're aware of them. We sense them intuitively, we see fragments of the future in what appears to be a dream or in a random thought that zips in and out of our conscious mind before we actually recognize it for what it is and see what it is really showing us. What if you could consciously become aware of the experiences in the future in this life and in your future lives to see how you're causing and creating them, and, at the same time, see how they're influencing your present life?

You already know how to see into the future and change your reality in the present as you simultaneously shape your future. You've done it every time you've envisioned something you want or daydreamed about an experience you'd like to have. You've traveled through time into the future by thinking about it, seeing yourself in the image of it, and feeling the experience in your mind. And then, as if by magic, at some time in the future what you've envisioned or daydreamed really happens.

What you've done in the present was to place your awareness into the future and experience the future in the present. In essence, you were following your future, instead of your future following the present. When the present catches up with the future, the energy vibrations are synchronized and you experience the future in the present. No magic, no mystery. Just what you thought was your imagination, but now it's your reality.

EMPTY ENERGY

Let's look inside the present to see into the future in this lifetime, to discover how the future shapes and creates the present, before we go exploring the future in another lifetime. When one of my editors suggested the idea for this book, I mind-tripped into the future to look at the possibilities of it. When I placed my awareness into the future, I became aware of a feeling that I could only term *empty energy*. I thought the energy was empty because there didn't seem to be anything there yet; I hadn't looked into my future thoughts, feelings, or experiences in relation to the book idea or tuned in to the energy that was associated with this book.

Once I got on course and began to explore the energy that was in the future inside this book, I saw that the energy wasn't empty. It only appeared that way because I hadn't looked into it completely and wasn't aware of everything that was in that future vibration of energy. When I pulled the future energy into the present, I realized that I hadn't been aware of the entire picture. I had only seen fragments.

By seeing only fragments, it's easy to think that the energy of the future is empty, that nothing is there yet. Even when we do see through the present into the future, it doesn't seem real because our feelings aren't there yet. When we put our feelings into the future images of our experiences and get in touch with them, the future becomes real in the present. When we consciously see all the pieces of the picture, we see that the energy inside future experiences is fluctuating, waiting for us to become aware of it and put it into motion, to set it into action in the present.

When I looked into the future fragments of the idea for this book, I saw that the energy for it was filled with lots of wonderful possibilities and even more probabilities, depending on what

I decided to do in the present with the energy of it, the direction I chose to take with it, and how I wanted to shape it. As I followed my future into the present, I brought the energy of this book from the future into my present and began to write it.

As I progressed through the present, day by day, page by page, into my future, this book felt very familiar to me, as if I were reading it while I was simultaneously writing it. The thought occurred to me that I'd written this book before, somewhere, someplace in time. More than just fragments existed in the future. When I first mind-tripped through time into the future in this lifetime, I'd subconsciously read the words that were already written while they were waiting for me to write them; I just hadn't been consciously aware of reading the words until I began to write them

If I'd waited for this book to just somehow "magically" appear in my present, I'd be no further along than I was when I first explored the idea, scribbled a few notes, and then meditated on it to look into the future energy of the book, to travel the interweaving threads. By waiting for something to happen that you've seen in your future, you're likely to experience the potential energy vibrations of the future moving around in cloudy circles, keeping the shapes and spaces of your future experience formless and floating.

You're stirring up the energy by looking into the future, but you're not giving it any direction to go, so the energy is just swirling around, seemingly going nowhere. It only appears to be this way. Once you put that energy into motion, you can consciously shape it in any way you want, directed by your thoughts and feelings, and followed by your actions. Then you're doing more than watching the energy and waiting for it to do something, seemingly all by itself without any help or guidance from you; you're reading the energy and moving it the way you want it to go. You're shaping and forming the future energy of your experience into your present reality.

INTERACTIVE EXPERIENCE: FOLLOWING YOUR FUTURE

You can be in your future in this life before you physically arrive there. You can make your future meet and match your present. Look into the swirling, forming energy that is filled with the vibrations of your future experiences to gather information, then put that future energy into motion in the present. It's like looking through a transparent, maybe misty, image of the future as the energy swirls around, becoming real in the future and the present simultaneously, with echoes in the past.

With the thought of seeing how your future shapes and creates your present, and to see what's already there, engage in an intuitive daydream or a focused meditation about something you'd like to have happen or would like to see occur in the future in this life. Choose something you're already involved in or emotionally connected to, because this is the thread of interweaving energy that you'll follow into the future and travel with to return to your present, to bring the future vibes into your present reality. You'll be looking into the energies of a probable future event in which you can change what seemingly hasn't happened yet in the future to correspond with your present and your past.

Whatever you choose to create, shape, or change already exists as malleable energy in the present and the future simultaneously. You can create the time frame in what appears to be the future for that energy to manifest in the present. As you energize the swirling mists of future energy with your intent, through your thoughts and feelings, whatever you envision becomes real.

Go through the swirling mists into the future to see the completed picture in your mind, then look back into the past, which is now your present, to see what you've done and what you're in the process of doing to bring the future, as you see it and want it to be, into your present reality. You may become aware of interconnected vibrations of past, present, and future energies that are already there. You may see how they interweave through this future experience as you bring it into the present. Follow your feelings and go with the flow.

After you've brought what you've seen in the future into your present, take another look into the future to see how it all happened in the past, which is your present now, between the time frames of now and then. You've changed the energies of both your future and present experiences that are connected to the future event. You've shaped and molded them into what you want them to be.

Be accepting of what you see and experience. Don't force anything; just be open to seeing and feeling how the interweaving energies of your future experiences vibrate and express themselves in both the future and the present. See your future experiences for what they are and for what they are showing you, and then bring the reflection of your future awareness into your conscious mind in the present.

You'll see how your future shapes and supports your past and present. Or maybe you'll see just the reverse: how your past and present have formed your future. If you see your future from this perspective, it's okay; linear habits can be resistant to change. You're probably very used to, and comfortable with, creating your reality and looking into your future from the present rather than looking backward from the future into the present.

From your present physical perspective, your future experience appears to be only a daydream because it doesn't exist yet; it's not real. Or does it exist now? Is it real through the energies of your interweaving thoughts and feelings about it? Because you've seen and shaped the future vibrations for it, your future experience *is* real. By putting your feelings into the picture and your thoughts into motion, by taking actions now to bring it to be, your future experience will happén, sometime, somewhere in the future from your present perspective. When the present catches up with the future, you'll see just how real it is.

Here's how my future experience became real, relating to writing this book: Once I got past the empty energy by looking into it and putting my feelings into it, I took the idea for this book further in the present. Instead of looking at the idea as a future possibility, I put action into it and made it come alive by beginning to write this book so I could physically identify with it more completely in my present. While I was in my future, I saw several images relating to this book happening in the present, instead of in the future. I saw this manuscript in the finished form of a book. I also saw a book contract being offered to me. At the same time, I saw my book being published.

None of this had happened yet in the present. The finished book was a probable future experience; it wasn't real in my present reality. It was a somewhat misty, transparent image—something that was in the process of happening, an idea that was shaping itself into being. I knew that my future was happening concurrently; it just hadn't happened in my present yet.

But then it did happen in the future, which is now my present. I was offered a book contract, just as I'd seen in my future vision. Since I'm writing this book now, am I creating my future, following my future, or doing both at the same time? Because I see this book in completed form in the future, where does this book really exist? As I'm writing this, it doesn't exist now in the present in the form of a book. Only a half-completed manuscript exists now. Does my future (the published book—the one you're reading right now) create my present (writing the book) and also my past (the idea for this book), or is it the other way around?

What do you think? What does your future meditation show you, and what does it say about your past and present? Are you beginning to see time as it truly is, magical and elusive, mystical and mysterious, slipping and sliding into and through your thoughts, your frame of reference, just like water slips through your hands, even though, a moment ago, you held it within your mind?

TEN

The Essence of Timelessness

How many times a day does someone ask you what time it is? Now I'm asking you. What time is it? It's a loaded question. Before you answer, simultaneously think about the answer to an unspoken question about space and synchronicity. Here's what I'd tell you if you asked me what time it is. "The time is now and the space is here." In reality, they're both nowhere.

In a linear vibration of time, the present can only exist if there's a past behind it or underneath it to support and create the present so the present can shape and build the future. Because we're all in physical form and therefore governed by physical laws, we tend to think of things in concrete, logical terms; but the nature of time is abstract. There is no beginning because there is no end. The past and the future exist together simultaneously, blending into the present to create an essence of timelessness. The present "now" is timeless. It incorporates the past and the future within itself. You have always been and you will always be. Your soul is immortal, eternal, timeless, and ever evolving into higher realms of awareness and enlightenment.

SOMEWHERE/NOWHERE

If your soul has always existed, where did your soul originate? You didn't just appear out of nowhere, did you? (The word *nowhere* is continually mispronounced. If you change where you put your emphasis, it literally means "now-here.") Neither did your experiences. Looking at a present frame of time in the here and now, the origins of your experiences were created somewhere before they were here; they were created somewhere, sometime in the past or the future, or at some other place and point in time. The energies of your soul—and the energies of your past and future experiences—created the present that you're experiencing now.

When you synchronize the vibrations of time with your experiences through the motions of past, present, and future energies —as you did in Chapter Six, in the tapestry meditation—it may seem as if you're in three different places at the same time, trying to see everything at once and being everywhere at the same time as the past and the future blur together into the present.

This is because you're trying to be in a static, non-moving place of *somewhere*, instead of being in a flowing, changing motion of *nowhere*. Center your attention into your experiences and clearly focus your spiritual awareness in the present to see the true nature of your soul and how your soul experiences time. Look inside your feelings in the here and now. All your experiences are timeless; you are *now-here*, living in the past, present, and future simultaneously, seeing your soul energies, and the energies of your experiences, synchronize themselves here, there, and everywhere at the same time.

Because we're physical beings experiencing life on Earth, we're governed by the physical laws of time. Our soul—our spiritual awareness—isn't. Inside the concept of simultaneous time, everything is all right here, right now. The ever-present here and now is timeless and all-encompassing. The word *timeless* is often defined as something that has always existed, that lasts forever.

We're all travelers through time, journeying through our many multidimensional experiences, some on Earth, some in other dimensions and realities of awareness. The here and now is timeless. Your soul is timeless. You can feel the vibrations of time and space by centering your awareness into your soul and synchronizing time and space so you can be here, there, everywhere, and nowhere at the same time. You can see and explore the energies of time and the energies of all your experiences in relationship to time. You can explore how your soul is centered in time. Eternity stretches far beyond what the conscious mind can reach, but your spiritual awareness travels easily through the eternal vibrations of time.

Some people draw a blank on the future the first time they mind-trip into it. This happens because they're coming up against their belief that the future hasn't happened yet. Other people view the future in a detached manner, and this causes the future to appear vague and misty. This is because you're not consciously aware of your emotions in the picture yet, and you could be viewing the scenes as if they are happening to someone else or as if they're not real. When you put your energy into motion by putting your feelings and yourself into the future, the future becomes as real as the present and the past. You probably discovered this in the previous chapter.

There also seems to be a bit of fear associated with facing the future. This is simply a fear of the unknown, a natural resistance to change. It's merely a trap, a trip-up designed by your conscious mind to get in your way. However, there might be something you've already experienced, or may experience the first time you venture into a future life, that I'd like you to be aware of and understand.

When you first try to place your awareness into a future life, you may enter what you perceive to be a hole of empty energy. You may have already experienced this in the previous chapter or in one of the other interactive explorations when you journeyed into the future. I experienced this hole of empty energy when I first explored the future vibrations of this book. It happens for two reasons: either because you're not in sync with the appropriate future energies, or because you believe that the future doesn't exist yet. The misplacement of your energies and/or your fear about going into something that you feel doesn't exist creates this hole of empty energy.

Some of my hypnosis clients and students, myself included, have experienced a void with a total absence of any physical or sensory sensations. This experience is very brief, but being prepared for it will eliminate the fear and help you get past it. Knowing what you might experience prepares you for it.

The void is totally black, without any light. Nothing seems to exist there. There's no sense of space or time or of anything. It's as if you don't exist in this space, as if nothing exists in this seemingly empty space. Remember that your belief is creating this, and your belief can un-create it. (This void is also sometimes experienced after physical death, when your soul separates from your physical body. It is created from your fear when you believe that your physical self is all there is.) There is no way to acclimate yourself to this void, because there is nothing there to identify with and there are no reference points to relate to. You may also experience this void as a tunnel or as a completely empty chamber in which you float, weightless and free.

You're in a space where the time vibrations of past, present, and future do not seem to exist. You're in the center of time, in which nothing exists and everything exists simultaneously. You're in the eternal, infinite, timeless moment of here and now. You've transcended time and physical reality. This is completely natural for your soul but it can be a little scary if you're focused on your physical consciousness. Your fear will pop you right out of this place, but if you can stay there for a while, you'll discover what time is really all about and how you create your Earth experiences.

Actually, this is an awesome experience when you get past your fear and start to explore where you are and what this space is all about. Within the center of time, the energies for everything exist; you can create and un-create whatever you want. You're between the vibrations of time, and the whole of time (no pun intended) is open to you. You can explore it to see what's there, what you can learn from it, and all the things you can do and create in this spiritual space. The first time you enter this space, it's totally black. But you don't have to go exploring in the dark. When you energize this space with white light—the light of your soul—you'll see all the vibrations contained within this sphere of no-time and no-thing.

INTERACTIVE EXPERIENCE: BEING HERE, THERE, EVERYWHERE, AND NOWHERE

Want to see what the black hole of time shows you? By purposely placing yourself in the middle of nowhere, in the still point in the center of time, you can travel through eternity, into and through the vibrations of time. You can look into the beginning and the end of time and see everything in between. Actually, that's a paradox; there is no end because there is no beginning. You can see the true nature of time; you can also see where and how your soul originated and why your soul was created.

> *Close your eyes and imagine yourself in complete darkness in the middle of time, in the middle of nowhere, in a place that didn't exist before you entered it. You may experience silence and stillness. You may feel as if you are suspended motionless. You may feel weightless or have a feeling of nothingness in which you seem to be nowhere. Actually, you are right in the middle of time— centered in the still point, in which everything begins and ends. You may also experience a feeling of emptiness as you go into and through the place of no-time, because you're between the vibrations of time.*
>
> *Go from blackness, nothingness, into a luminous white mist that appears gently out of the darkness to light your way through time. This white light is a vibration of universal energy that is similar to the energy vibration of your soul. Within the light, you*

see that you're between revolving points of energy that are moving around in various circular patterns and spirals of light. Take your time in this space to experience what the true nature of time is like. Just feel yourself floating comfortably, without any need to move, without any desire to go anywhere. Be in this space to discover what you want to know about time.

You may realize that being in the center of no-time is a paradox because you are actually here, there, and everywhere at the same time that you are nowhere. Since the nature of your soul is movement, you decide to create some waves in the fabric of time. You decide to go exploring to see where and how your soul was created and born. With that thought, you move through the vibrations of eternity, through the circles and spirals of white light, through the revolving points of energy, to see the birth of your soul. You can travel anywhere you wish through this sphere of timelessness.

As you experience the vibrations of time—and gather information about the true realities of time and your soul energies in this place of no-time that encompasses all the vibrations of time—you realize that in every moment of every existence, you're in a continuous motion of time and flow of energy as you create and experience every moment in every life. See, feel, and be in the center of time, in the middle of nowhere, in the center of everywhere, to discover all you want to know about the eternal vibrations of time. You see and know how and why your soul exists, and what it experiences through all the vibrations of time.

The next time you enter this space, it will already be energized with white light, with the light of your soul and the imprints of your thought energies and feelings. As you've discovered, this is a place of creation in which energy can be shaped and molded, created and un-created. This sphere of timelessness can be accessed at any time you want to go into and through the vibrations of time.

RHYTHM OF REINCARNATION

Now that you've traveled into and through time, above and beyond time, through the essence of timelessness, let's look at reincarnation as a trip through time. Your soul is eternal and returns to a physical form over and over again in a circular, cyclical pattern in revolving vibrations of time and energy. Your thoughts, experiences, and emotions are the connecting threads of energy that weave through every lifetime. Reincarnation is a cycle of birth and death, of simultaneous beginnings and endings, following a universal rhythm.

Some of the reasons we reincarnate are to balance karma, learn lessons, enjoy life, and evolve our soul. The whole idea is to gain knowledge, experience, and to become perfect; we do that through our Earth experiences and in our many multidimensional experiences. The purpose of life on Earth is to revolve through physical experiences and evolve our soul, to come full circle so that we completely understand all sides of our experiences on every level of awareness in every vibration of energy. As we come full circle, we see that the circle spirals in various directions—upward and downward, backward and forward, in a rhythm of movement that is in harmony with the energies of our experiences and the directions we take them in.

We get to see the whole picture when we're on the other side, when we're existing in the interim between lives as we're evaluating the life (lives) we've lived and deciding how to change our experiences during our next lifetime—whether it is a past or future lifetime—to balance our karma and choose what we want to experience and what we want to achieve as our soul's purpose that will help to evolve our soul. That's why we need to reincarnate, to create past and future lives in synchronicity with the present life we are living now and the experiences we are engaged in.

Another reason we reincarnate into physical form is because our soul desires the adventure of physical experiences in which we can grow our soul. If we're wandering around here on Earth in physical form, trying to learn our lessons, balance the energies of our karma, and live our lives the best way we can instead of floating around the universe flapping our wings, it's obvious we're not perfect yet.

Reincarnation is a timeless circle, repeating itself in ever-changing, revolving energies that spiral in many directions through universal cycles of birth and death, beginnings and endings. Our soul returns to Earth over and over again to experience both the good and bad karmic energies we've created. Karma is the connecting thread of energy that weaves through our experiences. If we don't balance our karma, we repeat versions of the same experience and revolve around in unchanged circles instead of evolving into enlightenment.

Reincarnation is a rhythm of movement between the Earth and the universe. The vibrations of time—past, present, and future—operate on the energies of a universal clock in a cyclic rhythm of movement, a fluid pattern of revolving motion. Look at nature and the seasons, with cycles of growth and dormancy, life and death. Trees lose their leaves in the fall and bloom again in the spring. With respect to reincarnation; our soul operates on universal time, with cycles of birth and death, beginnings and endings. Death is not an ending; it is a new beginning, a birth of our soul into another vibration of energy. When our soul enters a physical existence and we are born into a new physical body, we adapt our spiritual vibrations to the rhythm of Earth energies and physical time. However, our soul and our inner knowing continue to function on universal time. This is how we can access our spiritual awareness while we're in physical form.

Everything in nature and the universe is a perfect dance of harmony in tune with timelessness. Your soul is in tune with the rhythms of nature and the universe, following a circular rhythm and pattern. Your soul follows the universal Law of Balance. Even when you're in physical form while you live in the three-dimensional world of Earth, your soul adheres to the rhythm of the universe. Balance returns to itself, over and over. Day follows night, night follows day. The sun rises and sets. The tides of the ocean ebb and flow. The moon waxes and wanes. Look at nature, and how things occur in a circular, rhythmic pattern of cycles and revolving energies, and you'll see that balance and harmony are in all things. Your soul desires the same balance and harmony.

INTERACTIVE EXPERIENCE: ALPHA/OMEGA

There's no getting around it; you are a physical being at this revolving point and place in time here on Earth. You can explore the never-ending, always-beginning energies of time as they expand into eternity. Remember *The Time Machine*, discussed in Chapter Five? How would you like to have your very own time-travel machine? Instead of a clunky, metal, Earth-bound vehicle, you can travel through both universal and physical time through the vehicle of the screen of an Alpha/Omega computer—through the waves and frequencies of energy.

Picture in your mind an Alpha/Omega computer that contains all the information in the world, and in the universe, from the beginning of time until the end of time, which is sort of a contradiction because time is, was, and always will be. This computer is your time-travel machine. It has a special time-travel feature that operates on waves of energy. It can access information in what appears to be the past, the present, or the future.

You can use this computer to see pictures and stories of experiences in your past, present, and future lives. Type in a date and a place, or just one of the two, and pictures of your past-present-future lives will appear on the screen in full color with sound and moving images. Words appear as captions under the pictures, describing in detail what is going on. You can print out the words to show the complete stories of all the experiences in all your lives. If you don't know the date or the place, or you're just curious to see the interweaving threads of energy that link your experiences together, you can type in an experience or one or more of your emotions to see all the past-present-future energy expressions and connections.

Your computer has an easy-access feature similar to the help button on a toolbar. If you're not sure of the information you want or where to find it, simply type in a question mark (?) along with your feelings, and the computer will give you instructions on how to program and retrieve any information you desire.

Whatever you program this computer to do, it will do. It has a mega memory; it can retrieve your memories and show you pictures of memories that haven't happened yet. It can show you all the myriad possibilities and probabilities of your past-present-future experiences and how they change with your choices.

Now that you know a little bit about how your Alpha/Omega computer works and how to operate it, turn it on and try it out. Play with it, with all the buttons on the toolbars and the commands on the drop-down menus, to become familiar with it.

Use the time-travel feature to obtain any information you desire about experiences in your past, your present, and your future. You can go back to the beginning of time, whenever that was, to see how time started. You can travel through the eternal reaches and stretches of time to see how time continues through eternity and where your soul will be in all the multidimensional places in time. Your Alpha/Omega computer is your personal time-travel machine; it's powered by your soul.

Let me ask you again. What time is it? As you journey through timelessness within the energies of your soul, through the ever-present here and now, you may just come up with the answer to what time it is.

ELEVEN

Duplicate Dimensions

I f you think there's only the past, the present, and the future here on Earth, think again. In the infinite universe we live in, there are many other expressions of energy open to us. All you have to do is look for them in space and time. There's a lot going on in the myriad energies of your soul and the many multidimensional experiences you have. Look into a few aspects of your spiritual reality.

There's more to see than meets the physical eye. Look beyond the obvious and below the surface, into other realms of reality that your soul lives in simultaneously along with your lifetimes on Earth. Explore more familiar realities like dreams and déjà vu, then venture into duplicate dimensions and parallel lives.

There's a popular concept that we dream our life into being. We create our experiences in our subconscious mind, in our spiritual reality, before those experiences appear in our life; we also dream about what's going to occur before it happens. The catch is that most of the time we forget that we dreamed it; when the events occur, we're not consciously aware of having created and experienced those events before in a subconscious level of dreams. This concept goes a long way toward explaining feelings of déjà vu, because we pre-experience everything either in a dream state or in a spiritual level of mind.

Déjà vu is a sense of familiarity, of having seen or experienced something or of having been somewhere before. Déjà vu originates from both the future and the past. It is much more than it appears to be. Perhaps you've had what you thought was a precognitive dream about something that was going to happen in the future. Then the information that you previously became aware of or have already experienced in another level of mind, but have now forgotten on a conscious level, pops into your mind when a similar experience or feeling triggers it.

On the other hand, a feeling of déjà vu may surface as a memory of an event that occurred either in a past or future life without you being consciously aware that the event occurred in a previous or future life. It feels very familiar, but you can't quite place where you've had the experience before. Your soul remembers the event; this is what causes the feeling of déjà vu.

Déjà vu may not always be what it first appears to be. At times, it may feel as though you're actually experiencing the same things or similar scenes all over again. This is more than déjà vu and much more than a dream. It's a duplicate dimension of energy or a parallel place that your soul has lived in or is currently living in, and the memory or feeling of it is reappearing in the here and now—in your physical present.

You become aware of a duplicate dimension when the past and present interact simultaneously through a revolving point of energy. (You may have already discovered this when you traveled the light energies in the hole of time.) When you put future lives into the picture, there is another dimension, or realm, of the same dimension, like an echo that reverberates through a huge canyon of existence. With each and every variation of your experiences, there can be an unlimited number of duplicate dimensions or parallel experiences.

Before you go flying off in all directions, echoing yourself endlessly, let's be a bit linear about this. Think of one event in a past life as a duplicate dimension of energy that interacts with and influences your present life. When something in your present life triggers the past event, you're experiencing both dimensions at the same time, because the energies of the past-present event are in sync. This is how duplicate dimensions intersect in your present life.

Since you've opened up the avenue to explore the past in the present through the vibrations of a similar, karmic-connected experience, the energies of the past are experienced as a duplicate dimension in the present. Because the past and the present are now one and the same, vibrating at different levels of energy, you're more or less aware of both duplicate dimensions at the same time.

However, duplicate dimensions go much deeper and further than that. Your soul expresses itself in many forms. Being physical and living in the linear world of past, present, and future is only one of them. You're also experiencing life in nonphysical forms in your spirit body. Your soul exists as an energy form of light. This is easy to understand if you think about what your soul experiences and how it exists when it is no longer connected to your physical body.

For example, heaven and hell could be viewed as duplicate dimensions. How often have you thought that your life is a living hell, and, at other times, that your life is heaven on Earth? What if you're existing in heaven or hell at the same time you're walking around on Earth? What if heaven and hell aren't really places? What if they're an energy vibration of time and space that parallels what you're currently experiencing?

Your awareness and your experiences in a spiritual vibration of energy occur in a duplicate dimension concurrently while they're occurring on Earth in a physical vibration of energy. Very often, your physical experiences parallel the spiritual experiences that your soul is having. You can become aware of your nonphysical lifetimes and what your soul is experiencing when you tune in to your spiritual vibrations, in to your soul's awareness.

This brings up another interesting question. What do you do, and what do you think about, when you're not in physical form? Your soul, when not embodied in a physical form, still exists, because it is immortal. Do you just loll about the universe, drifting on a cloud in some sort of stupor or sleep until you reincarnate and come back down to Earth? I doubt it. The interim between lives is another dimension of your soul's existence where you have unclouded access to all your soul's knowledge, coupled with the information from all the lives you've experienced and are in the process of experiencing. Within this realm, you look into the past, present, and future simultaneously to choose and decide what you're going to experience the next time you incarnate. (See the soul-opening meditation on the interim between lives at the end of this chapter.)

While you're in the interim between lives, supposedly resting and rejuvenating from a past life before you reincarnate into your present life, your soul is also experiencing other lives in time frames of past, present, and future on Earth. While you're in spiritual form, you can share your spiritual knowledge with yourself; you can also influence and interact with various parts of your soul that are experiencing physical incarnations in different bodies with different names. (You've done something similar to this in Chapter Seven, when you met your past and future selves.) While you're in physical form this time around, you can access the spiritual information that you're privy to in the interim between lives by tuning in to your spiritual vibrations, by getting in touch with the essence of your soul.

While your soul is existing in the spiritual vibrations of the interim between lives, you can also interact with other souls still living on Earth. They're in a different dimension than you are; you're existing in the universe and they're still walking around, living and breathing on Earth. Have you ever had the experience of being contacted by a loved one who has passed on? If you have, then you know that he or she is aware of and can interact with certain experiences here on Earth. Oftentimes, loved ones who are no longer in physical form appear in our dreams to tell us of impending events. It seems that while they're in their spiritual form, they have easier access to the energies of those events. They also appear just to let us know that they're thinking of us and to let us know that we are loved.

Another aspect of the simultaneous time-space concept is that because all our past, present, and future lives are lived at the same time in different vibrations of energy, they exactly parallel, or are similar to, each other in feelings and experiences. This is because the interrelated energies of karma are woven through similar experiences. Remember the Old West scenario in Chapter Four?

A variation on the parallel-lives concept is that in addition to experiences in your present life paralleling experiences in your past and future lives, this also occurs on a spiritual-physical level. Your soul, in its nonphysical form, is having experiences along the lines of what your physical self is experiencing, except your soul's experiences are occurring in a spiritual dimension of energy while you are having the similar experiences in a physical dimension on Earth. This occurs because the Earth and the universe are mirrors of each other and because your soul's energies, being part of you, are intricately intertwined with your physical experiences. The things that your soul is experiencing in a nonphysical form, your physical self is simultaneously experiencing in its physical form. When you're in spiritual form, you're experiencing a similar existence in a replica of Earth.

This variation on the parallel-lives concept is similar to the philosophy *As above, so below*—as it is in the universe, so it is on Earth. This reflects how earthly and universal energy work together in harmony. It simply means that the Earth is a mirror of the universe, and vice versa. What happens on a spiritual, or universal, level also happens on a physical level in a different vibration of energy. Your physical self and your physical experiences are a mirror of your spiritual self and what your soul is experiencing in a nonphysical form.

You have access to all the information contained in your past and future lives, and in your parallel lives and duplicate dimensions, through your soul's awareness. Multidimensional realms of reality come into your awareness through your dreams and in your thoughts and feelings when spiritual energy interconnects and weaves through your present awareness. All you have to do is place your thought perspectives and image perceptions a little out of and above your physical consciousness and the way you view your present Earth reality. Look at your physical reality differently to encompass the true reality of your spirit.

SOUL-OPENING MEDITATION: BRIDGE OF LIGHT

You can journey beyond time and space into the nonphysical realm that your soul lives in when you're not here on Earth to see what your soul experiences in its pure energy form of light. You'll travel a bridge of light between the Earth and the universe, between the physical and the spiritual worlds, as you journey into the pure energy of your spirit, as you travel between both dimensions to see and know what your soul sees and knows.

You see a bridge in the distance that is shimmering and sparkling with ethereal energy, yet the luminous bridge appears to have physical substance and form. You know somehow that it bridges both the physical and the spiritual worlds—blending them and bringing them together. You've heard that there are bridges of light called rainbow bridges that span both the Earth and the universe, that give access and entry into nonphysical realms of spirit.

You notice that the physical and spiritual worlds are side by side, not above and below as you may have always believed. This seems a bit strange to you at first, then you realize it's perfectly natural, and you wonder why you never perceived it this way before. Both worlds vibrate together, a mere frequency or perception apart, yet they are simultaneous, each one intimately and intricately influencing and affecting the other.

As you walk toward the bridge, you notice that the vibrations of light that form the bridge are interwoven and in continuous motion. The sparkles and shimmers interplay with each other, creating a gentle movement, as if a soft breeze is flowing through the energy vibrations. You wonder what it would be like to walk upon this bridge. You notice that the bridge is perfectly formed, and that it rises up gently into an arch that connects the Earth with the universe. You see the handrails on both sides that have been formed with tendrils of luminous light.

You're not able to see where the bridge ends—it stretches into the universe far beyond what your eye can see. You wonder what is on the other side of the bridge, yet somewhere inside you, you know what's there. It's a recognition that waits to show itself, a remembrance that your soul holds deep within you. You walk forward more quickly, eager to reach the bridge and begin to travel it. You have a magical sense of what awaits you. A feeling of wonderful anticipation builds within you with each step. Finally you've reached the bridge. Putting your hand on one of the handrails, you feel a gentle flow of energy in your hand that circulates through your fingers and begins to move through your wrist and upward through your arm. The vibration of energy reminds you of what your soul is like in its spirit form.

Stepping onto this rainbow bridge of light between the Earth and the universe that spans and bridges together the physical and spiritual worlds, you notice that it's sturdy, secure, and safe. Even though it sways a bit, you know that it's the motion of energy that makes it move. You feel the gentle vibration of energy from the bridge that begins to radiate upward through your feet. It's the same gentle sensation you felt in your hand. You know that this is a magical, mystical bridge and that it can take you above the

Earth and across into the universe, above and across the physical world into the spirit world.

You again wonder what you'll find as you cross this bridge. But even as you wonder, you begin to remember more clearly; you remember what your soul is like in its pure, nonphysical form, when you were a being of energy, an essence of light. Moving forward to explore what is in front of you, the gentle vibration of energy reassures you and invites you to travel this bridge, this rainbow between the worlds.

Travel the bridge of light to see where it takes you into the world of spirit and what it shows you about your soul. Walk across the bridge to see what you'll find on it and on the other side. Perhaps you will see a spiritual guide who meets you halfway and offers to journey with you into and through this land of spirit. Perhaps you will see an angel who offers to guide you into and through the worlds beyond the bridge. Or perhaps you will choose to travel by yourself, guided by your inner knowing and soul awareness as you bridge the physical and spiritual worlds, to remember and reexperience what your soul is like and what it experiences in its pure, natural form of energy and light, and to bring both worlds together within yourself.

You are so much more than a physical being. You are a powerful, radiant, spiritual being of light. You can bring your spiritual awareness into every aspect of your life.

TWELVE

Tripping Through Time

Where will you live in your future lives, and what will you do there? What sort of experiences will you have? What souls will you be with that you're with now? You can trip through time into the future by placing your awareness into your next lifetime to see when and where you land and what you do—perhaps in relation to what you're doing now.

Your journey into the future will have pieces of your past lives tossed into the picture. You'll travel into and through the experiences in your past and future lifetimes that show you how these past-future experiences and their corresponding emotions relate to and are interconnected with your present experiences. Because of the simultaneous, synchronous nature of time, you'll see past and future events that have already happened and ones that are in the process of happening as the interconnected energies weave through them, much like how you traveled through the tapestry of your experiences in Chapter Six. You'll see past-future experiences as happening either together or separately. This will depend on your perception of the events.

You have several viewpoints available to you. You can be an observer and watch what occurs without feeling the emotions that are attached to the past or future experiences; you can be a participant and completely feel everything inside the past or future experiences; or you can do both at the same time. It will depend on what you're seeing and reexperiencing, and how you're responding to it. You will intuitively place yourself in the perspective that feels most comfortable and right for you; the one that will provide you with the greatest insight and understanding into your past and future memories.

Time moves in many directions—forward and backward, up and down, paralleling side to side, doubling within itself, going sideways, and looping around in circles as it spirals in a roundabout way through the energies of past-present-future experiences. As you journey through the vibrations of time into the past and the future, you'll become aware of and maneuver through revolving points of energy. These are the same revolving points of energy that you discovered in the hole of time in Chapter Ten and are also the pivot points, parallels, and polarities between your experiences—the interconnecting threads of energy that weave together past-present-future experiences.

A pivot point lets you travel in any direction through time— to move forward or backward, go up or down, to double or parallel, or to move sideways—by focusing your awareness into the central experience or emotion to see the parallels and polarities between the interrelated experiences and emotions, and to see how they are connected through karmic energies. The parallels in your past-future experiences are the similarities in the past-future situations. The polarities show you what is not yet in balance.

To keep yourself centered, and to give yourself a reference point, think about a current situation in your life. This is also a pivot point; it will provide you with the direction and drift to maneuver through time to see how, where, and why your current experience originated. Once you've seen the beginnings, follow the interweaving energies into the present to see how the energy vibrations of this experience affect you now. See how your present experience was influenced by what occurred in the past, how it has affected and influenced the future, or how the future influenced and interacted with your present and past experience.

This will give you answers, understanding, and insight into why you're experiencing what you're experiencing now, because you'll see how and why events in your past and future lives influence and affect present situations and feelings. You'll also know why you created certain experiences or chose to partici-pate in them. This helps you understand your present experi-ences better and to know how to balance your karma from past and future events.

During your trip through time, since this is an interactive exploration, you can influence the energies you become aware of. You can change events in the past and the future to correspond with how you want them to be reflected and expressed in the present. You can also change the energy expressions of present experiences as you see them reflected in both the past and the future. You already know how to do this because you've done it before in Chapters Five and Six. As you are involved in past-future scenes, you can balance the energies of your karma while you are there. You will intuitively know how to do this as you see beyond what occurred in the physical experience, through your spiritual awareness and understanding.

If you come across anything that is hurtful or painful, you can rise above it into the white light of the universe. If you remember from Chapter Seven, this white light is safe, peaceful, and pro-tecting. It will keep you from feeling the hurt or pain and will also help you balance any and all negative energies, as well as heal all parts of the experience. Know that you've created all the experi-ences in every lifetime to help you evolve your soul. Karma is always a good, positive thing, even when it appears to be negative, because it offers you the opportunity to grow from the experience and to grow your soul into enlightenment.

Also be aware that you chose to experience your karma in the manner in which it occurs. Accepting responsibility for your karma, for your actions, gives you the power to change it, to turn it around into a good, positive experience. As you balance your karma, whether you do it in the past, the future, or the present, it's very important to balance it sincerely from your soul, to honestly change negative feelings into positive ones. This heals the experience, because there are no remnants of negativity left.

Some of the things you may discover, in addition to experiences in your past and future lives that are lived on Earth, are how your soul functions in a nonphysical, spiritual form, as well as an increased understanding of how your soul functions in a physical body. You may become aware of past and future lives in duplicate dimensions and parallel places. You may trip into multidimensional worlds and parallel lifetimes spanning the reach of past, present, and future simultaneously. Let yourself explore the full depth and range of them. Shift your focus and area of perception; open up your awareness to completely experience them.

You'll be traveling through the vibrations of time by placing your thoughts and awareness somewhere other than in the present. This is also known as mind projection, in which you project your awareness outside yourself and the immediate present. You've done this before in all the interactive exercises and meditations in this book. When you travel into a past or future memory, the past-future event that you're seeing, feeling, and experiencing becomes more than a memory, because you're opening up and exploring the energies of it. You're pulling the past-future energies into your present awareness; it becomes an experience that you see and feel on a very real level within your mind and soul, even though it occurs in another place, in another time.

You may experience many different feelings as you travel through time and space. One is a feeling of disorientation from where you are and who you are now in the present. This is a natural occurrence when you place your awareness and attention outside yourself, and as you travel on your soul energies. Other feelings you may have are that you are flowing with the energies, and you may feel as if the energies are directing you, rather than you directing them. This is your soul guiding you. Go with the flow of what you are experiencing.

You may also feel as if you are outside of your body; this is fairly normal when your awareness is expanded and you're in tune with higher, spiritual energies. When you access higher realms of energy, you may astral project as you travel through time. You may have already done this when you traveled the rainbow energies in Chapter Seven to meet your past and future selves.

You may feel a slow, smooth, rhythmic sensation as if time and space are in slow motion and you're in the center, or you may feel just the opposite—as if you are in the center of a whirling vortex of energy. You may also feel as if you're gently drifting or rapidly spinning; this is due to the rate at which your awareness is traveling through the past-future energies. All of these feelings are natural, normal, and comfortable. You may feel some or all of them to varying degrees, or you may just experience an expanded sense of awareness.

Words can only take you so far; your mind will take you wherever you want and need to go to see the important events in your past and future lifetimes. There are so many variables as to what you will experience that it's best to follow your own inner guidance. On your journey, you're free to explore the realms and realities of your past and future lives in all of their many multidimensional vibrations.

MIND-EXPANDING MEDITATION: A TRIP THROUGH TIME

As you trip through time, take your time—as much time as you need—to journey through the energies and vibrations of all the events and emotions your soul is experiencing. Your soul knows that there isn't any past or future, even though those words will be used; there are just other synchronous experiences your soul has had, is in the process of having, or will have in its many multi-dimensional travels.

Take a deep breath in and let it out slowly. Breathe in and out naturally as you let your entire body relax. Feel your body relaxing as you breathe in and out slowly and naturally. Feel all the muscles in your body letting go of tension and tightness, becoming more and more relaxed with every breath you take. Feel yourself becoming calm and quiet, relaxed and peaceful within yourself. As your body relaxes, your mind opens up and expands; you become more spiritually aware as you enter a meditative frame of mind. You become more aware of your soul and its travels through many lifetimes.

Just breathe naturally, in and out, in a rhythmic manner. You feel completely comfortable and wonderfully relaxed, entering a calm, peaceful place within yourself. There's no rush; there's no such thing as time, there's only breathing and being relaxed, feeling very peaceful within yourself as you open up your mind's awareness, as you open up the wisdom of your soul.

Take another deep breath in; feel your breath entering your body. Pay attention to how it feels. Breathe out, feeling your breath leaving your body. Pay attention to how it feels. Pay attention to how you feel as you're breathing. Listen to the sound of your breathing as you breathe naturally and deeply, in and out, in a gentle, rhythmic motion. Feel your breathing and how your body responds as you breathe. Just breathe. Your body is completely relaxed now, and your mind is completely open and aware.

As you're breathing in and out, naturally and comfortably, imagine that you're on a sandy beach on a pleasantly warm, beautiful summer day, watching the waves as they come to the shore and as they return to the ocean, listening to the ebb and flow of the tide. This place, this day, this moment is absolutely perfect, and you feel a wonderful sense of contentment and peace being here. The sun is warm and pleasant on your body, and you feel a gentle breeze that caresses you softly.

See and feel yourself there in this safe, soothing, peaceful place on the beach on the most beautiful day you've ever experienced. Take a few moments to be there, to look around you, to see what is in this beautiful, warm, safe place. Take some time to enjoy being there, and to be in tune with the energies and harmony of this place. Walk around to find a spot on the beach where you feel most comfortable and in tune with your energy vibrations. Breathe as you sit down on the soft sand and relax even more on this beautiful beach.

You feel so relaxed and comfortable here in this peaceful place. You're in tune with the harmony of the waves and in harmony with yourself. The sound of the water is peaceful and soothing, relaxing you more and more. You decide to lie down on the soft sand of this beautiful beach, resting on the warm sand as you listen to the motion of the waves and watch the blueness of the sky above you. You notice a few puffy white clouds in the sky that are just floating along. You feel so in tune with them; you're just floating along in a comfortable rhythm and motion of harmony. Your spirit feels free and light, as free as the clouds that float above you. As you're breathing in and out, you continue to watch the clouds in the sky floating by.

Take another deep breath in, feeling it fill you completely. As you let it out very slowly, you know that your breath is like the ocean with waves of time coming and going, matching the rhythm of your breath as you inhale and exhale. As the waves ebb and flow, you breathe in and out. Listen to the waves as they come up to the shore and as they recede into the ocean. Listen to the sound of the waves as you breathe in and out, as the waves of time ebb and flow. You're breathing in and out, breathing in a natural rhythm and flow that is in harmony with the tides, breathing in harmony with the ebb and flow of time.

As you breathe in, you feel your spiritual essence expanding with your breath, becoming lighter than air. You feel very free and open, expansive and light. As you breathe out, you feel your spirit leaving your body, floating freely and easily away from your physical body, traveling on your breath, floating through the air, just like the clouds floating leisurely along in the beautiful blue sky above you. You feel your spirit—your soul—freeing itself from your physical body and the bonds of the Earth. You feel weightless and free. You feel so weightless and free that your awareness —your spirit—begins to float upward toward the clouds in the sky. It's a safe, comfortable, natural feeling, as natural as breathing and listening to the sound of the waves.

You feel so completely relaxed and peaceful as you see and feel your awareness—your spiritual essence—continue to float upward, slowly, bit by bit. Your spirit seems to expand and rise on your breath as you breathe in and out. Your breath cushions you like a gentle current of air as you rise higher and higher. Breathe in, breathe out, in a gentle, rhythmic motion. Breathe in, becoming lighter than air. Breathe out, floating on a soft current of air.

As you're floating through the sky, you become aware of a soft radiant white light that is filtering through your mind as you enter one of the beautiful white clouds in the sky. As you breathe in the light, you're aware of your soul, and you see yourself looking into and through a mirror of time, reflecting past and future images, flowing into a timeless realm. You feel your mind—your soul—flowing into a vast, infinite sea of white light, an essence so ethereal and luminous that words cannot describe it. See and feel this gentle, illuminating energy as it bathes your body and your mind with the higher wisdom and eternal essence of your soul. Breathe this light inside you; feel it circulating in and through your body, your mind, and your soul.

As you feel the gentle, warm, somewhat effervescent energies of white light softly bathing your mind and gently circulating through your body, you become completely aware of your soul and you know that you are an eternal, spiritual being. You know that your soul is timeless. You're aware of the freedom you have to go beyond the limits of your physical consciousness, beyond the restrictions of physical time and space. You know that you can go anywhere in time and space, into any past, present, or future experience simply by placing your awareness and attention there. You know that time and space are illusions of physical reality. In the multidimensional energy of your soul, time and space do not exist. You know that your soul is part of that infinite essence of light that is beyond time and space.

Breathe in and be in the light. Be and become one with the light. Be and become one with your soul. Be the light; be your soul. Breathe out the light and feel it expanding all around you. Breathe in the light and feel it expanding within you. Breathe.

Within the ethereal essence of white light, you see a guide who is waiting to help you travel into and through the vibrations of time. You experience a wonderful feeling of complete trust and feel a positive attunement with your soul guide. Your guide is part of your soul and knows everything there is to know about all your experiences in your past, present, and future lives. Your inner guide will show you events and emotions in your past and future lives and will explain how they interconnect with and weave through the experiences in your present life to give you a complete understanding of those experiences. As you travel through time, your guide will show you how the energies of past, present, and future blend together.

Your guide says it is time to begin your journey, and asks if you are ready to explore the experiences and emotions in your past and future lives. As you answer, you move toward your guide to reconnect with the essence of your soul. Your guide knows that you are ready to see what you've done in the past and the future, to see what you have yet to do in the past and the future, and to understand how all your experiences are intertwined and how they affect one another, how they vibrate in a synchronous movement with one another, each experience affecting and influencing all your interrelated experiences.

Your soul guide reaches out to you. As you embrace, you merge your physical and spiritual energies together. As you take the hand of your guide, you feel yourself floating through time, floating through a vast infinite sea of time. Your awareness is floating, flowing through the ethereal essence of light as you travel into and through the infinite reaches of time—going into time, through time, beyond time, above time. Your awareness is in a place of luminous light, a light that is alive and vibrating with energy, with the essence of life. Your awareness is flowing and floating gently through this light, through the vibrations of time as you begin your journey with your soul guide, who will show you the experiences in your past and future lives and how they interconnect with the experiences in your present life.

Breathing in and out, feeling expansive—lighter than air and floating on a gentle current of air—you feel the essence of your spirit rising up even higher into the air, above the clouds in the sky. Your spirit is expansive and light, and can travel anywhere you wish. You flow through the vibrations of time with your soul guide—seeing, knowing, and understanding all the things you see and experience. Breathing in harmony with your spirit, your awareness travels on the energy of your breath.

You feel yourself soaring, gliding, rising even higher in the air. Floating freely in the air, you observe the world below you. Your guide asks you to look at the Earth—the home where your soul resides now. You see a great expanse of ocean below you. As you watch the waves ebb and flow, you feel the rhythm of the tides, the rhythm of time, as you breathe in and out. You see the various shades of blue in the ocean; you see the ripple of the waves and the white foam. You feel the gentle current of air as you float above the vibrations of time, above the energies of the Earth.

You rise up into the air far above the Earth, looking at the beautiful blue-and-green Earth below you, revolving slowly in the universe. You see the majesty of the heavens and the panorama of the universe. A feeling of timelessness surrounds you; you know that time, as you normally perceive it, does not exist for your soul. You notice that your vision and awareness are also expanded. You see places on Earth that have a special connection for you in the future, places where you will live in your next lifetime. These places call to your spirit, beckoning you to visit.

As the Earth slowly revolves below you, you feel your spirit being drawn to a place on Earth where you will live in another time in the future, a place that has a special reason and purpose for you to explore now, a place that will provide you with meaningful information that you can bring back with you into your present life. Your soul guide travels with you as your spirit floats easily and softly on a gentle current of air into the place your soul will call home in a future lifetime.

As your spirit explores this physical place on Earth in the future, you have an expanded view and an increased understanding of all the things that happen here in your future life; you know why they happen, how you've created them, and why you chose to experience them. You know and understand the purpose your soul desires to achieve in this future life. You see souls that you know now, who are also with you in your future life here. You see the interactions between you, and you become aware of the karma that needs to be balanced as the future blends into the present. Your soul guide shows you the whole picture of the experiences in your future life, and explains why and how you're creating them in the present to experience them in this time frame of the future. You see how the present and the past are interwoven with the future through the threads of time.

Take your time to see what occurs in the future life you are experiencing here and to understand why it happens. Listen to your soul guide as your inner knowing—your spiritual awareness—speaks to you through your thoughts and feelings as you observe and participate in the events and emotions that are part of your future life here. Completely explore your future experiences to see how they affect your present life. If there is a need and you want to, you can balance your karma in the future now, to make everything right, or you may choose to bring the karmic energies into your present life and balance your karma there through your current experiences.

When you're done exploring everything you want to know about your future life here, your spirit rises into the air above the Earth with your soul guide. You again notice how the green-and-blue Earth slowly revolves below you. If you want to, you may visit another location where you'll live in the future or the past that has a special meaning and purpose for you to be aware of now. Explore the experiences you see there to understand why they are occurring and how they're interwoven with your present and your past. You may visit as many places as your soul desires for you to see and experience.

When you're done with your trip through time, you feel your spirit rising into the universe above the Earth as your soul guide accompanies you. You feel your essence return to the ethereal, luminous white light, and you're aware of being in this infinite sea of white light. Your guide takes you into the multidimensional energies of your soul to show you where you live when your soul is not experiencing a life on Earth. Explore this land of spirit; remember what it is like to be a completely free spirit. Reexperience what your soul knows. See what your soul shows you. Listen to what your soul says.

Be there for a while in the light, in this land of spirit, in the home of your soul, to reflect on everything you became aware of about your past and future experiences, and what you discovered about the vibrations of time and your simultaneous, interconnected experiences. Talk to your guide to ask any questions you may still have or to reach a higher understanding of all that you have experienced on your trip through time.

While you're in this very spiritual vibration of pure awareness and knowledge, look at the situations and events you created for yourself to have and experience in your present life, and to understand why your soul desires to experience them.

When you are done with your reflections and you're ready to return to what your physical self perceives as your present reality in this lifetime, bid your soul guide good-bye. Thank this wonderful guide who showed you the experiences your soul has had and will have, who gave you insights into your soul and provided you with answers as you saw the events and emotions in your past and future lives, and in the multidimensional realms of your spirit. Your guide embraces you and gives you a special gift to bring back with you into your physical reality. Watch your guide go into the pure essence of white light, knowing that you may call upon your guide at any time you want or need to, and for any reason.

When you're ready to come back down to Earth, you turn your attention toward Earth and see again the great expanse of ocean below you, moving in a natural rhythm and harmony with both the Earth and the universe. You slowly and gently float down into a beautiful white cloud in the sky. Your spirit travels on your breath, returning to your physical body, returning you to the place here on Earth that you call home now.

Gliding gently back down to Earth, you land softly on the sand of the beach where you began your journey through time. You see the ocean and hear the waves as they move in rhythm and harmony, as the waves of time ebb and flow. You feel the breath of your spiritual essence as you breathe in and out. You hear the rhythm and harmony of your soul, in tune with the natural flow of the Earth and the universe. Breathing in and out, you bring the full awareness and understanding of your soul and all that it has experienced in your travels through time into your conscious mind.

As you reorient yourself into the present here and now, slowly bring your awareness into the present time by focusing and directing your thoughts and feelings into who you are and where you are right now. Bring with you the insight and understanding *of all that you have experienced in your past and future travels. Take some quiet time to re-vibrate your spiritual energies into the physical here and now, knowing that you've just taken a sacred journey into your soul.*

This time-tripping experiential journey that you've just taken offers you unlimited opportunities to travel through time. You can take this trip through time into the multidimensional realms and realities of your soul as many times as you wish. Every time you journey into the past and the future, you'll become aware of more information, and you'll understand more about your soul and how it travels through the energies of time.

THIRTEEN

Reevaluating Reincarnation

A re your past and future lives a whisper of wind blowing
through time, a heartbeat somewhere in space? Or is reincarnation a reflection of time and space in the multidimensional worlds and realities within your soul? You can
reevaluate the original definition of reincarnation that was
presented in Chapter One in terms of the experiences you have
explored within this book, within your mind and soul, and within
your past, present, and future lives.

The past, the present, and the future are an essence of thought,
an ethereal wisp of energy that flows softly by you and touches you
gently on a whisper of the wind inside your soul. The spaces of
matter that your soul exists in simultaneously touch you in a poetry
of movement and awareness. No matter what the definition of
reincarnation is, one truth remains constant: Your soul is immortal
and journeys through the multidimensional realms of your experiences in vibrations of the past, present, and future in the eternal,
infinite reaches of time. Every lifetime offers a wonderful rebirth

of your soul into ever-evolving, always-expanding, higher levels of awareness and enlightenment.

Dare to look at life differently. View the energies of your soul in the here and now; explore and expand your awareness. You can make the future really happen—right here, right now. Inside the vibrations of time and space, you have the power to make all your past, present, and future lives everything you've always wanted them to be—and more.

Index

Praise for Irene Hannon's Heroes of Quantico Series

Against All Odds

"Award-winner Hannon debuts the Heroes of Quantico series with a wonderful array of believable characters, action and suspense that will keep readers glued to each page. Hannon's extraordinary writing, vivid scenes, and surprise ending come together for a not-to-be-missed reading experience."

4½ stars Top Pick, *RT Book Reviews*

"I found someone who writes romantic suspense better than I do. This is a captivating, fast-paced, well-written romantic suspense destined for my keeper shelf."

Dee Henderson, author, the O'Malley Family series

"Well-drawn bad guys, a dysfunctional relationship between Monica and her diplomat father, and witty male banter between Coop and his partner Mark add intensity and levity in equal measure in this rapid-paced, well-written romance."

Relz Reviewz

"Hannon delivers big time in this novel. The intercontinental suspense plot combines flawlessly with a fantastic romance that sizzles. The realism in her FBI details adds authenticity to the novel and allows the book to branch out to a male audience and women who would not pick up a romantic suspense title. The characters are all well developed, and the interplay between partners is wonderful."

Book of the Month, *The Suspense Zone*

An Eye for an Eye

"RITA–award-winner Hannon's latest superbly written addition to her Heroes of Quantico series neatly delivers all the thrills and chills of Suzanne Brockmann's Team Sixteen series with the subtly incorporated faith elements found in Dee Henderson's books."

Booklist

"Hannon continues to bring her own special brand of suspense and romance to this genre. This winning recipe provides readers with characters that are engrossing, a plot filled with unexpected twists, and a love story that will melt your heart. The only downside to this terrific novel is that you won't want to put it down."

4½ stars Top Pick, *RT Book Reviews*

"You will be hooked from the first chapter with an explosive start, followed by brilliant pacing through the rest of the story and the perfect balance of suspense, action, and romance."

Relz Reviewz

"A new queen of suspense joins the ranks of Brandilyn Collins, Terri Blackstock, and Dee Henderson . . . her name is Irene Hannon. This is masterful storytelling."

Deenasbooks Blogspot

In Harm's Way

"A fine-tuned suspense tale. RITA–award-winner Hannon is a master at character development, writing believable, three-dimensional characters. Fans of Dee Henderson will enjoy this book."

Library Journal

"Fast-paced crime drama with an aside of romance . . . and an ever-climactic mystery. Hannon's tale is engagingly sure-footed."

Publishers Weekly

"A well-plotted thriller and a spectacular romance. Hannon is clearly on track to lay claim to the title 'Queen of Romantic Suspense' in the CBA market. *In Harm's Way* is the perfect blend of suspense, balanced with just the right touch of romance between two leads who have so much chemistry the sparks practically fly from the page. Masterfully plotted and crackling with romantic tension, *In Harm's Way* delivers the goods."

Booktalkandmore Blogspot

"*In Harm's Way* kept me turning pages as it raced from one twist to another. This book will be a hit with Irene Hannon fans!"

Susan May Warren, RITA–award-winning author